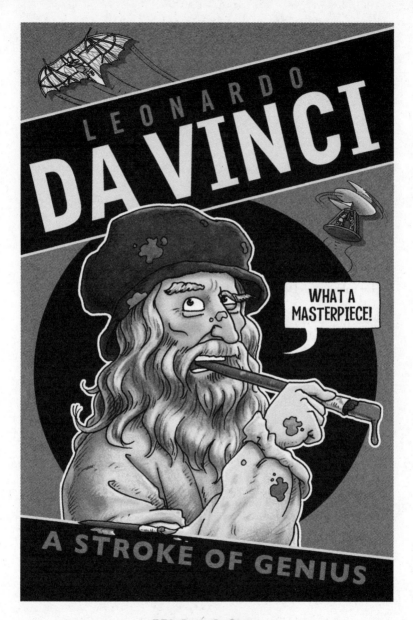

Michael Cox
Illustrated by Clive Goddard

SCHOLASTIC

Scholastic Children's Books,
Euston House,
24 Eversholt Street,
London NW1 1DB, UK

A division of Scholastic Ltd
London ~ New York ~ Toronto ~ Sydney ~ Auckland
Mexico City ~ New Delhi ~ Hong Kong

First published as Dead Famous: *Leonardo da Vinci and his Super-brain* in the
UK by Scholastic Ltd, 2003
This edition published 2019

ISBN 978 1407 19261 1

Printed and bound in the UK by CPI Ltd, Croydon, CR0 4YY

2 4 6 8 10 9 7 5 3 1

CONTENTS

INTRODUCTION

Millions of people know Leonardo da Vinci as the Italian artist who painted the most famous painting in the world, the *Mona Lisa*.

Millions more regard him as the light-years-ahead-of-his-time scientific genius, mathematician and engineer who dreamed up designs for helicopters, tanks, submarines and terrifically tidy toilets, hundreds of years before anyone else ever got round to creating the real things.

Other people think of Leo as the wiser-than-a-think-tank-full-of-masterminds who searched for the human soul, drew fantastically beautiful and detailed pictures of the most mysterious and complicated bits of the human body, and was forever trying to work out personkind's place and purpose in our huge and complex universe.

Others regard him as the musician who made his own instruments, wrote his own songs and performed them beautifully in front of awestruck audiences.

And, believe it or not, a whole load more people perceive him as an architect, map-maker and town planner who devised astonishing schemes for stunning new super-cities, buildings and waterways.

The astonishing thing is that *every one* of these people is right! Leonardo was *all* of these things and more! If they'd had careers teachers in the fifteenth century, advising him on what job he should go for would have been a complete nightmare. He was fascinated by just about every subject under the sun (not to mention quite a few beyond it). During his 67 years Leonardo ended up turning his super-brain to more projects than most normal people could fit into a hundred lifetimes...

And, in addition to being ace at so many different subjects, Leo also appeared to have everything else going for him! He was incredibly handsome, a snappy dresser, as fit as a fiddle and really good at sport. In fact, he was said to be so strong that, using just one hand, he could twist a horseshoe out of shape. He was an expert horse rider and a brilliant fencer, but he was also a pacifist, so he never drew a sword in anger (but he did draw quite a few in charcoal). On top of all this, he was a brilliantly witty and entertaining  chin-wagger who had opinions and ideas about almost everything. And, even more amazingly, he never went to a proper school!

In this book you can find out all sorts of fantastic facts and stunning stories about the man who is generally thought to have been one of the brainiest and most creative people who've ever lived. Like...

- Why he threw a bucket of water over a priest.
- How he almost scared his dad to death.
- What he did to make his art teacher give up painting.
- What he did with human skeletons and lengths of string.
- How he planned to drown a whole army.

You can also read about his incredible inventions that were hundreds and hundreds of years ahead of their time. And there are all sorts of drawing tips from the man himself, a guide on how to paint a masterpiece and a lesson in how to speak 'Artalian'. And, if all that isn't enough to get you drooling like a dehydrated Doberman, you can also check out what Leo might have written in his legendary Lost Notebook and find out the great man's innermost thoughts about the world, life and minestrone soup.

Leonardo once said...

*Wanting to know things is natural to all **good** people!*

So it's time to jiggle *your* grey cells, engage *your* thinking tackle, and get the low-down on da Vinci and his super-brain!

NATURE BOY

Leonardo da Vinci was born in Italy at 10.30 p.m. on Saturday, 15 April 1452, quite near the fortified hilltop village of Vinci. Wow! What an amazing coincidence! Not! Actually da Vinci isn't a surname it just means he was Leo of Vinci village.

Leonardo's mum, Caterina, was a 16-year-old servant girl and his dad, Ser Piero da Vinci, was a notary (sort of a solicitor, but without the big flash car and laptop PC). Although she was obviously quite fond of him, Caterina wasn't actually married to Leonardo's dad and, in the year that Leo was

11

born, Ser Piero married another 16-year-old girl, called Albiera, who was loads posher than Caterina. Then, not all that long after that, Caterina got married to someone far less up-market than Ser Piero, leaving little Leonardo with his dad and stepmum.

However, as Ser Piero and his new wife were forever nipping off to nearby Florence on business and whatnot, they had very little time for Leo. So, despite having multiple mums and dads, the little lad eventually ended up spending lots of time with his grandma and grandpa in Vinci and passing his days in the company of his dad's younger brother, Francesco, whose job was to look after the da Vinci family's olive trees, orchards and vineyards (and spare children).

As Leo grew up, he and Uncle Francesco passed many happy, sun-filled hours wandering around the local area. The village of Vinci overlooks the valley of the River Arno and much of the hilly countryside around it is stunningly spectacular, with superb streams, awesome orchards, perfect pools and wonderful woods. All of this gorgeous natural beauty is said to have deeply affected Leonardo. It gave him an appreciation of nature that would remain with him for the rest of his life. As Uncle Francesco checked out the da Vinci vines and olives, little Leo would constantly be asking his uncle all manner of questions about the cute critters that chirruped and squeaked and grunted in the hills around them.

Although not a lot is known about Leonardo's childhood he's generally believed to have been so knocked out by the local landscape that he soon began wandering off on his own, sketching trees, rocks and animals. One of his earliest drawings is a picture of two ducks on a pool, which he is thought to have drawn somewhere in the vicinity of Vinci.

As he grew up Leo soon got into the habit of always carrying his pencil and sketch-pad with him wherever he went, drawing whatever caught his eye, in much the same way people nowadays carry cameras and are forever snapping splendiferous scenery and fascinating folk. Leonardo continued this habit throughout his life. His notebooks were incredibly important to him because they allowed him to record his ideas, questions and observations about all the amazing stuff he saw and dreamed up while it was still fresh in his mind ... *before* it was all replaced by a whole load of amazing *new* thoughts!

He also began to make notes about the best ways to improve his artistic skills. Here's what he said about making rapid sketches of people...

Learning with Leo

Speed-drawing people: Quickly draw the main lines their bodies make but ensure you keep it simple. Do an 'O' for the head and straight or curved lines for the legs, arms and trunk (main body – nothing to do with elephants).

Then, when you get home, finish off your sketches properly.

Developing rapid hand-eye coordination: Make some silhouettes out of cardboard in different shapes, then throw them from a high place and quickly draw the various movements and new shapes they make at several points during their fall. This will improve your hand-eye coordination no end!

It wasn't just drawing that young Leonardo became skilled at as he grew up in the Tuscan countryside. By the time he was a teenager he'd become a dab hand at decoration, too.

THE STORY OF LEONARDO'S STUNNINGLY SCARY SHIELD

ONE OF THE PEASANTS ON THE DA VINCI ESTATE CARVED HIMSELF A SHIELD OUT OF WOOD FROM A FIG TREE. HE FANCIED GETTING IT DECORATED SO HE TOOK IT TO SER PIERO

CRAFTY SER PIERO IMMEDIATELY PASSED THE SHIELD TO LEONARDO

DECORATE THIS MANKY SHIELD WILL YOU, SON

SURE, DAD. NO PROBLEM!

COULD YOU GET THIS DECORATED BY ONE OF THEM THERE POSH PAINTERS IN FLORENCE, BOSS? I'LL MAKE IT WORTH YOUR WHILE!

NO PROBLEM! BUT IT'LL COST YOU A TROUT AND A WILD BOAR

THE SHIELD WAS A RIGHT DOG'S DINNER, ALL WARPED AND MANKY. BUT, BEING A PRACTICAL LAD, LEONARDO STRAIGHTENED IT UP, GOT IT POLISHED, THEN COVERED IT IN HIS OWN SUPER-DUPER VARNISH

THIS IS FUN! I LOVE A CHALLENGE

HE THEN SET ABOUT THINKING UP A SUITABLY SCARY IMAGE TO GO ON IT. FOR INSPIRATION HE COLLECTED A LOAD OF DEAD LIZARDS, BATS, CRICKETS AND SNAKES, AND OTHER WEIRD CREEPY-CRAWLIES

YEAH... REALLY GROSS!

HE THEN TOOK LEONARDO'S SUPER-SHIELD TO A MERCHANT AND FLOGGED IT TO HIM FOR HEAPS OF DOSH

OOOH! VERY NICE!

DOSH

AND THEN THE MERCHANT TOOK THE SHIELD TO THE DUKE OF MILAN HIMSELF AND FLOGGED IT TO HIM FOR A SMALL FORTUNE! MORAL: NEVER TRUST A SOLICITOR!

MORE DOSH

Learning with Leo

Feeding your imagination: In order to stimulate your imagination and get yourself feeling really creative and bursting with ideas, look at a wall covered with shapeless stains. If you look hard enough you will see fabulous mountain landscapes, terrific trees, bloody battles, fantastic faces and strange costumes (on the other hand, if you're hopelessly unimaginative ... you'll probably see a wall covered with shapeless stains).

YEUCH!

So Leonardo continued growing up and wandering around the sunny Tuscan countryside, eating lots of minestrone soup (his favourite nosh), being constantly fascinated by the never-ending mysteries of science and nature, and no doubt dabbling in lots more arty projects and whatnot. During this time it's generally believed that, rather than going to school like kids do nowadays and swotting for his SATs, Leonardo was educated by the local priest who taught him important stuff like not to chew the end of his quill, the 3Rs, and why it's not a good idea to blow your nose whilst shaking hands with a nobleman.

And then, around the time Leo was getting pimples the size of Mount Vesuvius and sprouting hair in really scary places, his dad decided to move from Vinci permanently and take his super-bright son with him. So, at the age of 15 or thereabouts, Leonardo da Vinci, whizz-kid and world-famous-hairy-genius-in-the-making, flitted to the most happening and exciting city in all of fifteenth-century Europe ... fabulous *Florence*!

THE RIP-ROARING RENAISSANCE

Depending on which century you happen to be living in, Florence is a day's gentle donkey ride or an hour's terrifying taxi trip from the village of Vinci.

Florence had once been a dangerous and disease-ridden place but, by the time Leonardo and his dad moved there, it had become a fabulously wealthy city, buzzing with excitement, activity, new ideas ... and *really* big mosquitoes! It was filled with mega-rich merchants and all kinds of terrifically talented creative types and you couldn't walk five metres without tripping over an artistic genius or bumping into a big-cheese businessman. As a result, much of the civilized world regarded Florence as the most happening, cutting-edge, where-it's-at city on Earth.

One of the main reasons Florence, and one or two other European cities, were regarded as such happening places was that, during the century or so preceding Leonardo's birth, a big change had begun to take place in Europe and it affected the ways in which people thought, behaved and lived their daily lives.

This big change is now known as the all-doing, all-thinking, all-enquiring, rollicking, rip-roaring Renaissance!

In order to understand how Leonardo played his part in this exhilarating era of learning and creativity you may find the following guide helpful…

Rough guide to the Renaissance

Around about 500CE, after the ancient Roman Empire had collapsed, all sorts of wild and smelly barbarian tribes began rushing around Europe, generally being vulgar, violent and disagreeable. During this turbulent period in history, fisticuffs, famine and fecklessness were widespread and Western Europe entered the 'Middle Ages', as they later became known.

The Middle Ages (or medieval times as they're sometimes called) weren't *all* gloom and doom though, and when the barbarians settled down a bit some really cool art was created, including groovy Gothic cathedrals, superb stained glass, tasteful tapestries and magnificent manuscripts. And, what's more, universities, hospitals and banks were all medieval inventions. But, generally speaking, people were superstitious and ignorant and things relating to human progress and well-being just didn't tootle along at the rate they did in some other eras.

The Middle Ages lasted until around the fourteenth century when, comparatively speaking, things began to look up. Certain places, especially Northern Italy and the Low Countries (now known as Holland and Belgium), started to become prosperous and peaceful.

This more settled atmosphere led to the arrival of a new age of discovery and creativity, which was eventually named after the French word meaning rebirth: in other words ... the *Renaissance!*

The Renaissance is now regarded as one of the most important times in European history because it was when thousands of ignorant, nose-picking, wheel-kicking thickwits were transformed into educated, enlightened, sensitive types who were just fizzing with need-to-know-can't-wait-until-tomorrow interest and excitement about the world they lived in. Previously, people had thought things like:

But during the Renaissance people started thinking things like:

So, all of a sudden, learning, enquiry and discovery became the new stupidity, apathy and ignorance! And this is what happened next...

1 Renaissance brainy types began looking back to the days of the ancient Greek and Roman civilizations, and said things like:

2 Scholars began to be influenced by what the wise bods of days-gone-by had written about politics, life and law, while arty types began to take long and thoughtful glances at classical plays, poetry, sculpture and architecture and were inspired to create great new art of their own.

3 Artists began to have new thoughts about the way they made their art and what their art said about their subjects.

4 There was a real spirit of enquiry in the air. Suddenly, people wanted to know everything about everything! Science! History! Nature! Art! Stuff like:

5 As well as finding out about their immediate world they were also desperate to find out about the great big world that lay beyond their own front doorsteps. Explorers such as Vasco da Gama and Christopher Columbus weighed anchor and set sail to discover the astonishing places that lay over the horizon.

6 Merchants got really busy buying and selling things, often to and from people living in the countries that had been discovered by the seafarers. People who lived in the towns and cities became much better off. They wanted to spend their dosh on all the fancy goods that were arriving from far-off places. As a result, the wheeling-dealing merchants grew really rich. Which meant they had stacks of spare

cash to spend on art, architecture and sculpture! Especially art and stuff dedicated to the glory of God (because it made them feel far less guilty about being so ridiculously rich).

7 In the middle of the fifteenth century, Johannes Gutenberg developed Europe's first printing press in

Germany. Before this, books had been few and far between because they'd been written out by hand, just one at a time. By the time Leonardo was in his late forties there were about a thousand printing presses operating in Europe. This gave lots more people the opportunity to learn to read and write.

Astoundingly smart, talented and inquisitive, young Leonardo couldn't have wished for a better time or a better place to begin his career as all-round genius than fifteenth-century Florence.

Leonardo's Lost Notebook 1469

March
My country bumpkin days are finally over. I have moved to the wonderful city of Florence. This place is huge and is teeming with all kinds of interesting people, many of them dressed in fine clothes and riding lovely horses. All a great feast for my eager eyes.

I ♥ horses!

There are educated and talented creative types all over this fine city! And many from foreign lands, too, all here to do business and admire the great art. Yesterday I saw the fantastic dome on the cathedral, designed by our great Florentine genius, Brunelleschi.

Cupola of the Duomo

There is so much to take in here that my brain is positively fizzing with excitement! I also saw one of the Medici yesterday; probably Lorenzo. They're the top family here in Florence. Papa does work for them and says they're definitely the guys to be in with. They're very wealthy!

April
Papa has decided it's time I learned something useful. But what am I to do? Momma and Papa weren't married so I'm

not allowed to be a solicitor, or a banker, or a doctor or pharmacist, so there's no point in me going to Florence Uni to learn Latin, geometry and law. Instead, Papa's arranged for me to train to be an artist at one of the most creative hothouses in the city: the studio of Andrea del Verrocchio. I will be living there with ordinary young men: the sons of butchers, bakers and pasta makers. Which suits me fine; just as long as I'm learning and drawing and being creative. And I'm not at all bothered about not being taught about geometry and things. I can find out about those things for myself later on! I start at A del V's tomorrow. Can't wait!

When it came to knocking out awesome art, Andrea del Verrocchio was the bee's knees. Bigwigs and hot-shots from far and wide came to his studio to commission all manner of magnificent masterworks.

Verrocchio's

...for the finer things in life
Fab frescos, furniture, sculptures
and paintings! Cool carvings,
memorials, banners and coats of arms!
Gorgeous goblets and salvers
(gold or silver on request)!
Macho military machines and armour!
Yes, we have gotta the lotta...
plus some terrific terracotta!
You commission it! We make it!
No jobba too big or small!

Vinci
FLORENCE
NOWHERE
ELSE

Andrea del Verrocchio (1435–1488)

When Andrea was a young lad, something happened that was to affect him for the rest of his life. One day, he and his pals were larking about, chucking lumps of rock, when a stone he'd thrown accidentally hit another boy on the head. Unfortunately the stone killed the lad and Andrea was arrested for murder. However, after a few weeks in prison, he was let out – accidental deaths were very common in Florence in those days. But the memory of this terrible tragedy remained. Many years later, when he was working on a sculpture of David (the sure-shot who slew Goliath), he gave him a sword instead of a stone and sling because he felt so bad about his terrible misdeed.

When Andrea grew up he became a goldsmith's apprentice and learned to do all sorts of snazzy stuff, including carving precious stones, designing jewellery, and working with molten metals. He eventually became a sculptor and painter and in 1464 he got the job of making a tombstone for one of the mega-rich and all-powerful Medici family. It was the big break he needed. After that he became their official sculptor, jobs came pouring in and his business really took off!

Verrocchio's workshop

Verrocchio's studio in Florence was a hive of activity with artists and apprentices all working their socks off. In those days artists weren't the trendy, windbag, no-talent posers (that some are reputed to be nowadays) but were real, hard-grafting craftsmen who had to learn every skill and trick of their trade in a

long and arduous apprenticeship that could last for up to ten years. And artists' studios weren't the pretentious, no-talent, poser hangouts (that some are reputed to be nowadays) but were more like top-notch factories where teams of skilled and dedicated craftsmen turned out beautiful art that was meant to be admired and to last for all eternity.

The daily grind

There were similar artist's studios like Verrocchio's on almost every street in Florence and in every one of them young men like Leonardo were learning skills such as drawing, painting, sculpting and goldsmithing. During their first year at these studios, the lads were known as *discepolos* and were generally treated as dogsbodies who fetched and carried for the older artists. Amongst their duties, they were expected to:

1. RUN TO THE SHOPS

OY! HANG ON A MINUTE! I HAVEN'T TOLD YOU WHAT TO BUY YET!

2. HEAT THE GLUE AND VARNISH

I SAID **VARNISH**, NOT **VANISH**, YOU STUPID BOY!

3. CLEAN THE PAINTBRUSHES

PREFERABLY WITH A RAG!

4. SWEEP THE FLOORS

WITH A BROOM! WITH A BROOM!

Whilst the *discepolos* were flitting around the studio they would see the master craftsmen and artists doing their stuff and pick up tips as they dashed this way and that. Whenever they got a spare moment they practised improving their own drawing skills.

After their first year, the boys became known as *garzoni* and began developing the techniques they needed to master in order to become a fully fledged artist.

These included things like:

1 Learning to draw folds in fabric

This was very important; many of the apprentices would be making their living from painting religious pictures with biblical figures dressed in cloaks and robes that fell in intricate folds around them. These folds made gorgeous shapes and shadows, which were a delight to the eye when painted well. In order to learn this skill the apprentices copied drawings by his master and made sketches of fabric drapes, which had been specially stiffened with plaster so that the folds wouldn't drop out.

2 Preparing art materials

If you wanted to knock off a quick masterpiece in Renaissance times there was no nipping down to the local branch of Art Materials R Us and picking up half a dozen tubes of colour, a canvas and a couple of brushes. All brushes, paints and painting surfaces had to be made in the studio. So the lads were expected to:

Grind the pigments

Pigments are the raw materials that give paint its colour. In Renaissance times they were made by crushing things such as rocks and earth to create the brown colour known as ochre, or by grinding semi-precious stones such as lapis lazuli to produce the brilliant blue colour called ultramarine (meaning *from across the seas*, because it was imported to Italy from Afghanistan). However, some pigments were obtained from other natural materials. For example the bright red colour known as carmine was made from squidged cochineal beetles.

Make paintbrushes

To produce soft brushes, apprentices tied together bunches of hairs taken from the tails of weasels, stoats or ermine (an up-market sort of weasel). They then slotted the hairs into the hollow quill of a bird's feather and stuck a wooden handle into its other end.

Hard brushes were made from pigs' bristles, which were then softened up by being used to whitewash walls.

Prepare wooden panels for painting on
The wooden panels the artists painted their pictures on were first boiled in water to prevent them from splitting. Next they were coated in size, a sort of glue made from animal skins. Finally, to give them an even surface for painting on, the panels were coated in gesso (a mixture of chalk and water).

3 Becoming dab hands at daubing
If the lads looked as if they'd got what it took they'd be entrusted with more and more important bits of work, like painting in the buildings, trees or figures in the background of a commissioned painting. To do this they

needed to be familiar with the two main painting methods used in Renaissance studios:

Egg tempera painting

In tempera painting, pigments are mixed with water and egg yolk. Tempera paint dries very quickly so if the artist makes a mistake they have to paint over it.

Oil painting

Oil painting had been introduced to Italy from the Low Countries during the fifteenth century and would gradually replace tempera. In it, pigments are mixed with a raw oil such as linseed to give a rich colour. This means the paint is slow to dry and mistakes can be easily wiped off.

And, as if all that wasn't enough to keep them rushed off their feet, the boys would soon have to get to grips with a newfangled and quite recently discovered artistic skill. It's a painting and drawing technique that still gives artists problems to this day. Well, as they say, the main thing with any sort of problem, be it artistic or otherwise, is to keep it in ... perspective.

2-D OR NOT 2-D?

Drawing and painting in perspective was one of the hottest new skills in fifteenth-century painting. During his time at Verrocchio's, Leo would have had to learn to master the art of painting and drawing using this exciting new technique.

Before the Renaissance, most artists hadn't a clue how to make their pictures and the objects in them look three-dimensional. If you look at medieval pictures, like the famous tapestry of the Battle of Hastings, all the figures look rather like cardboard cut-outs because they've been painted (or stitched) two-dimensionally. This is because the average Middle Ages daubers had no idea how to represent perspective in their pictures. Perspective is the phenomenon (and optical illusion) by which things seem to become smaller the further away they are.

If a medieval artist painted someone small in a picture it was usually because:

a) that person wasn't at all important in terms of their status in society; or

41

b) they really were small – but it normally wasn't because they simply happened to be standing in the distance.

In the early Renaissance, artists, architects and other talented types began linking their knowledge of art, maths and science, and eventually came up with the idea of perspective. Some time later, painters learned the knack of creating the impression of space, distance and solidity on completely flat surfaces. These were some of the techniques they used to create these effects:

1 Clever use of light and shadow to give objects a more rounded form. This is the technique known as 'modelling'.

2 Use of the artistic trick known as foreshortening. In other words the illusion whereby objects appear to be *shorter*, but actually aren't.

MY ARMS ARE REALLY THE SAME LENGTH BUT MY LEFT ONE APPEARS TO BE SHORTER BECAUSE OF THE ANGLE FROM WHICH YOU ARE VIEWING IT

3 Use of perspective. This is the phenomenon by which the edges of regular shapes, such as walls and roads, follow lines that converge, then meet in the distance at a spot known as a vanishing point.

SEE HOW THOSE TRAIN TRACKS ALL MEET IN THE DISTANCE? THAT'S PERSPECTIVE, THAT IS

WHAT'S A TRAIN TRACK?

Around 1426, an artist called Masaccio painted a picture on a completely flat church wall in Florence. It featured Jesus on the cross, with God and the Holy Ghost, and was known as the *Trinity*. His use of perspective gave onlookers the impression that they could actually put their arms around the subjects or even walk into the scene and stand between them.

It sounds hard to believe now but fifteenth-century people were probably as astounded by this new art technique as mid-twentieth-century people were when they saw their first colour TVs or heard their first stereo records.

THIS NEW PERSPECTIVE THINGY IS UTTERLY GOBSMACKING!

Leonardo got so excited about the thrilling idea of perspective that he mentioned it in one of his essays. However, along with stacks more of his essays, this piece of writing has since been lost. (It probably went in the wash with his smock.)

Scope for improvement
Leonardo once said…

The youth ought first to learn perspective, then the proportions of everything.

So it's no surprise that he became really fussy about accuracy in his pictures and getting his subjects to look as lifelike as possible. In order to make sure he was really spot-on with things like details and perspective *and* to make the job of painting and drawing easier, he designed a handy art aid, which he occasionally used for checking the composition and proportions of his pictures. It is now generally known as a perspectograph, but Leonardo called it his trellis-work.

It consisted mainly of a grid of guidelines made from cotton threads. This was held vertically, then viewed through an eyepiece set about 30 cm away from its centre. When you looked through the grid at whatever you were intending to paint you would see the whole image divided into equal-sized squares.

Leo's said to have recommended using the grid in various ways including the following:

a) Draw a grid of the same proportions on a sheet of drawing paper then draw what you see through the eyepiece one square at a time until all the squares are filled (or someone shouts 'Bingo!').

b) Make a drawing using a freehand style, without the use of an art aid, but then use the trellis-work to check the accuracy of your work.

Learning with Leo

How to look at things: Look at just *one* detail of the scene. When you've got it firmly fixed in your brain, move on to the next detail and do the same.

Keep doing this until you've got a complete picture in your bonce.

Leonardo wasn't the only bright spark in the studios of Florence. There were loads of other talented young artists, like Botticelli, who would one day become famous and successful, though not nearly as famous as

Leonardo – otherwise you'd have heard of him, wouldn't you? (Oh, you *have*... beg your pardon!)

Sandro Botticelli (1445–1510)

Sandro was an apprentice at the studio of Filippo Lippi at the same time as Leo was learning with Verrochio. His real name was Alessandro di Mariano Filipepi but he was nicknamed Botticelli, which means 'Little Barrel'. Leonardo liked Botticelli and thought he was a good laugh as he was forever cracking jokes and goofing around. However, he didn't think much of his painting and said that he thought the backgrounds in Sandro's pictures were a bit naff and that he ought to pay more attention to perspective.

Like lots of other hot young artists doing their thing in Florence at this time, Sandro later created masses of brilliant art for the Medici family, including one of his most famous paintings, the *Birth of Venus*, which shows Venus, the Roman goddess of love, emerging from a giant clam shell.

Sandro also painted lots of religious pictures, including the *Madonna Magnificat*, and the *Madonna of the Pomegranate*, (and Madonna, the Final Farewell Concert).

He also worked on the decoration of the Sistine Chapel in Rome, but only did the walls, having decided to leave the ceiling to the artist Michelangelo (who had much longer arms than him). When Savonarola, the religious fanatic (see page 128), was powerful in Florence in the 1480s, Sandro suddenly, and quite amazingly, had his own attack of religious fanaticism, too, and began painting pictures that were really, *really* religious (but this was obviously just a coincidence).

Leonardo and all the other apprentices were improving their artistic skills with each hour that passed. But Leo would be the first to create the piece of work that was so stunning it almost reduced his teacher to tears...

LEONARDO A GO-GO

Leonardo's Lost Notebook 1470-1471

1470

I'm as busy as a bee at the studio. There's so much to do and see and I'm learning new skills with every day that passes. We're working on a massive bronze ball to go on top of Brunelleschi's dome! It's six metres across and weighs over two tons!

Verrocchio's got us doing all sorts of mathematical calculations and scientific experiments to discover the best way to attach the ball to the pointy lantern tip.

We're also trying to work out how to support it, the best place to fix the chains that will keep it in place, and just how strong winds will affect it once it's up there. All that sort of thing is completely fascinating! As far as I'm concerned science and art are inseparable, they really do depend on each other.

Science ⟶ Art

February 1471

Verrocchio's so pleased with my progress that he's made me his second-in-command. So life is great! When I'm not working, I'm out enjoying myself, playing and listening to music and strutting about in my trendy pink clothes (having decided that pink is the ultimate colour for cool threads!). In the studio I've been learning about creating special-effects machines for pageants and plays. Apparently old Brunelleschi was a dab hand at conjuring up skies full of living creatures and flashing lights. I've made a dove that goes up and down a string. (Well, I am only an apprentice! I'll get round to the really spectacular stuff later.) And we're busier than ever.

The Duke of Milan is coming to visit next month and Lorenzo dei Medici wants him to be flabbergasted by fabulous Florence!

15th March 1471
The Duke visited yesterday. And what a parade we put on for him!

I reckon his Dukeness must have been well impressed!

27th May 1471
Today they hoisted our big bronze ball on to the top of the dome using this brilliant crane on rails which Brunelleschi rigged up years ago. I thought it was so fantastic that I made these drawings of it.

51

Be an angel and paint that cherub for me, Leo

In 1472 Verrocchio was doing a big Baptism of Christ painting that had been commissioned by some monks to hang on their monastery wall. It showed Jesus standing in the River Jordan while St John the Baptist tipped water on his head and a couple of angels knelt at his feet. Verrocchio decided that Leo was now competent enough to work on a big, important project so he asked him to paint one of the angels. When he finally got round to checking out Leo's angelic artwork, he received a terrible shock.

Verrocchio was as sick as a parrot because Leo's superbly painted angel completely outshone his own artwork and he immediately vowed to give up painting for ever.

How to speak 'Artalian'

One of the things that art experts often refer to in Leo's angelic contribution to his master's painting (and lots of his other pictures for that matter), is his use of the painting technique known as *sfumato*. This is one of several words that people use when talking about Leo's paintings and the other amazing art that was created in the Renaissance. Being the keen and intelligent reader (or pretentious twit) that you are, you will obviously want to regularly drop these words into your conversation. So, for the purpose of impressing your teachers, liberally splashing your

friends with fresh saliva and frightening your pets, here are five friendly explanations and pronunciation guides for some common 'Artalian' terms you may wish to use.

Sfumato (pronounced 'sfoomato')
Sfumato is an Italian word meaning smoky, or hazy. Earlier painters had used hard lines, or edges, to pick out and define shapes in their pictures, but Leonardo often preferred to gradually blend his colours so that shapes became indistinct or blurry, as if seen through a veil or cloud of smoke. This gave his pictures a slightly mysterious atmosphere. He also used the *sfumato* technique for the landscape backgrounds in many of his paintings, which added to the feeling of perspective that so many of those Renaissance artists were nuts about. If you actually go outside and look at a real landscape you may notice that as things recede into the distance they do

actually become less clear, especially on hot, shimmery, summer days (or if you've left your specs in the caravan).

Chiaroscuro (pronounced 'kiaroskooro')

Chiaroscuro is the technique by which Leonardo gave shape to objects in a picture by picking out light and dark areas to create contrast and that 3-D effect that is so essential to achieving a sense of perspective. Leo once said that: '*Chiaroscuro* is the soul of painting.'

Exaggerated *chiaroscuro* can create a really dramatic feel, a fact now recognized by modern film and TV producers who often use artificial lighting to give a scene real oomph and kerpow!

Cartoon

When Renaissance artists created cartoons it didn't mean they painted angels zooming through the clouds with the word 'WHOOOOSH!' trailing behind them in huge red letters, or David splattering Goliath with a big 'KERSPLATTT' sign and a speech bubble saying 'TAKE THAT, LOFTY!'

In Leonardo's time, cartoons were the perfectly serious drawings that artists made as a preparation for the creation of some stonking great masterpiece. One of Leonardo's most famous cartoons is *Mary, Christ, St Anne and the Infant St John*, which he drew in chalk on paper. It can now be seen in the National Gallery in London.

Fresco

Fresco is the Italian word for 'fresh' as in…

This wall-painting technique involved slapping water-based paint onto areas of partly-dried plaster.

Contrapposto

Contrapposto is the positioning of human figures to give lots of curvy, lifelike attitude with their legs and arms pointing one way and their heads interestingly tilted in another, instead of being drawn all stiff and straight.

Not long after Leo had painted his divine angel, Verrocchio decided that his 23-year-old star pupil was now skilled enough to become a master of his trade and he was made a member of Florence's numero uno artistico A-team ... the Guild of St Luke. After all those years of study and practice he would now be able to set up in business on his own and show the world what he was made of.

Renaissance Florence's guildy complex

Everyone in Florence was incredibly proud of the world-famous arts and crafts that were created there and they wanted to maintain the highest possible standards in their city's output of gorgeous goodies. So, if you wished to produce and sell these things, first you had to complete a long training, just as Leonardo had done, after which you'd hope to gain entry to a guild. Belonging to a guild told your prospective customers that you could be trusted to produce work of the highest possible quality and that there was no chance of this sort of thing happening...

There were 21 of these guilds, or *arti* as they were known, and any professional who was anybody belonged to one of them. Their members consisted of all sorts of people, including cloth merchants, wool merchants, silk weavers, bankers, spice merchants, fur traders and, of course, artists and crafts people! The job of Leonardo's organization, the Guild of St Luke, was to make sure its painter members didn't get up to dodgy practices such as, for example, substituting cheapo azurite blue pigment in a painting for the far superior and more expensive lapiz lazuli.

If a door's worth doing, it's worth doing well

Everything the artists and craftsmen of the guilds did had to be spot-on. If it wasn't, they weren't happy bunnies. Their aim was to create the most beautiful objects imaginable, even if it took them a lifetime!

In 1401, the artist Lorenzo Ghiberti (1378–1455) began making a set of decorated doors for the northern side of a building in Florence known as the Baptistry. He finished them 23 years later, when he was 48.

The moment Lorenzo finished his divine doors he was given an exciting new career opening and was commissioned to begin work on a pair of doors for the *eastern* side of the Baptistry. He finished those 27 years later, in 1452, when he was 73!

The sculptor and poet, Michelangelo, described Lorenzo's lovely doors as…

Wonderful enough to be the Doors of Paradise.

Despite the fact that creative types like Leo, Botticelli and Ghiberti could generally paint and carve away to their art's content in relative peace and quiet, things in fifteenth-century Florence weren't always sweetness and light. Not far beneath the glittering surface of Florence (and the rest of Italy for that matter), all sorts of plotting was taking place. And many of these undercover shenanigans led to terrible scenes of mayhem and slaughter, as you'll soon discover…

THE DISUNITED STATES OF ITALY

Throughout Leonardo's life, Italy wasn't the sunny, united, boot-shaped country it is today. Well, the shape and weather were much the same, but Italy definitely wasn't a country, and it definitely wasn't united!

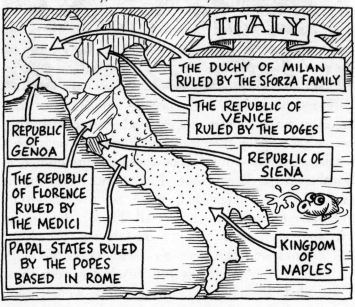

ITALY

THE DUCHY OF MILAN RULED BY THE SFORZA FAMILY

THE REPUBLIC OF VENICE RULED BY THE DOGES

REPUBLIC OF GENOA

REPUBLIC OF SIENA

THE REPUBLIC OF FLORENCE RULED BY THE MEDICI

PAPAL STATES RULED BY THE POPES BASED IN ROME

KINGDOM OF NAPLES

The area was divided into separate mini-countries, or city-states as they were known, each of which was ruled by one all-powerful city. At the end of the fifteenth century there were about 14 city-states and each one was controlled by a few powerful individuals and families who were constantly cooking up sinister schemes to nobble neighbouring city-states and waste their worst enemies (and you thought the Mafia was a modern invention).

Throughout the Renaissance the city-states of Italy frequently went to war with each other. And when they weren't scrapping, they were cuddling up to each other whilst secretly devising double-deals, or forming alliances with countries like France, Turkey and Spain in the hope that they might help them zap their city-state rivals. Trying to keep track of all the complex Italian city-state shenanigans would make following the plot of a TV soap seem like a piece of cake (or a cake of soap?).

Some of the most powerful city-states were those controlled by Florence, Milan and Venice and consequently these were the places where Leonardo spent most of his life. His whole existence was linked with the fates and fortunes of their various rulers because they had the power to make or break his career, simply by offering him a huge commission, recommending him to one of their mates or, far less helpfully, spreading the word that he was a complete duff-budgie.

More often than not, Leonardo's role was that of a sort of Renaissance Mr Fixit whose job was pleasing whichever top tomatoes happened to be in power. He would paint them pictures, design them buildings or use his inventive talents to dream up military schemes to help defeat their enemies in war.

Naturally, as his life was so closely connected to theirs, he was often witness to much of the skulduggery and savagery that took place between these big players in inter-city-state stakes.

While he was in Florence it was the all-powerful Medici he had to bow and scrape to.

The mega-rich Medici

The Medici (pronounced 'medeechee') clan was definitely the wealthiest and most powerful family in town. Because of the family name (the Italian for doctors) it's generally thought they'd initially worked in the medical profession, but over the years they'd become richer and richer and had eventually ditched their doctoring duties and become merchants and international bankers.

Lorenzo de Medici (1449–1492)

Lorenzo de Medici was only 20 when his father died and he and his kid brother took over ruling Florence. Lorenzo was a real go-getter of a Medici, not to mention a bossy-boots. He was good at football, wrote poems and songs, loved hunting and playing practical jokes and always dressed in cool threads. He also spent lots of money on partying and art ... and partying.

Giuliano de Medici (1453–1478)

Like his brother, Giuliano was a bossy-boots and a big spender but he never got to be as a big a tyrant as Lorenzo, due to meeting the following sticky and extremely unpleasant end...

THE FLORRYGRAPH

26th April 1478

MEDICI MURDERED AFTER MASS!

Florentines! Today, just as the bell rang to signal the end of mass in our lovely cathedral, the treacherous but fabulously wealthy family, the Pazzi[1], and their evil cronies, charged in and tried to murder our very own Lorenzo de Medici with poisoned daggers. Lorenzo was stabbed in the neck but his servant gave it a big suck and got the poison out. Quite tragically his younger brother, Giuliano, was killed by Bernardo Baroncelli, a member of the Pazzi gang!

There followed a scene of total chaos with screaming crowds and galloping horses all over the place, but in the end the guards caught nearly all the murderers. A rope was put round the evil Pazzi's neck and then he was thrown out of a high window. He was closely followed by none other than the Archbishop of Pisa! Yes, *he* was in on the assassination attempt, too! And, most oddly, as the two of them were gasping their last gasps, the Archbishop suddenly whirled around and took a great big bite out of Pazzi's chest!

1. The Pazzi were the other big European banking family of the time. If this took place today it would be like the bosses of Barclays trying to murder the directors of NatWest in St Paul's Cathedral.

Leonardo's Lost Notebook 1478

27th April 1478

Yesterday's murder in the cathedral really was a spectacular affair! By chance I was passing by when it all happened. And naturally, I rushed around drawing the action and the excited and horrified faces that were all over the place. It was too good an opportunity to miss!

30th April 1478 Bit quieter round here today. Turns out that the argy-bargy in the cathedral was a result of the Pope falling out with the Medici over money and then backing the Pazzi in their plot to murder Lorenzo and Giuliano.

2nd June 1478

Most of those treacherous cathedral conspirators have been hunted down and executed now. About 100 of them altogether. And the very gory remains of their bodies have been paraded

around town as a warning to anyone else who might be thinking of trying to overthrow Lorenzo. I'm feeling a bit disappointed, actually. I was hoping the Medici would commission me to paint a big mural of the execution on the front wall of the prison. But Botticelli got the job! And he's getting 40 gold florins for it! He's also got the job of painting a portrait of Giuliano de Medici (before his murder, that is). Ah well, such is strife!

THE FLORRYGRAPH
18th December 1479

MEDICI MURDERER FINALLY GETS HIS COME-UPPANCE!

Following the carve-up in the cathedral last April, they hanged Bernardo Baroncelli, the swine who killed our beloved Giuliano de Medici, today. Apparently, after committing the murder, he hid in the cathedral, while everyone else dashed around like headless chickens. Then he got on his horse, escaped over the border and hopped a ship to Turkey. However, thanks to our esteemed Lorenzo offering a reward for his return, dead or alive, the Turks caught him and sent him back. And now, quite deservedly, he's as dead as a doornail!

Leonardo's Lost Notebook 1479–1480

18th December 1479

I watched them hang Bernardo Baroncelli today. It was really interesting! For his deadly dangling, Signor Baroncelli wore a small brown cap and a blue coat lined with fox fur and trimmed with red and black velvet bands, teamed with a very fetching black serge jerkin and black tights. Dead stylish! (I do like to note these details). As I've said so many times before, if only you open your eyes there is much to see in life (and death for that matter). I also managed to do this sketch of him while he was jerking and twitching on the end of the rope. As he

was thrashing about so much I got the angle of the head a bit wrong so I drew it again, just to be sure.

Oh yes, and in the meantime Lorenzo's taken the Pope's nephew prisoner. I've a feeling there'll be more trouble soon!

6th January 1480

Uh oh! The man who delivers my minestrone has just told me that Florence is now at war with the Pope! But he says Lorenzo's pulled a fast one! He's managed to get the King of Naples on his side. So, in view of his smart move, everyone's now calling him Lorenzo the Magnificent. Phew! Italy seems to be controlled by a load of two-faced triple-crossing crooks and power-mad maniacs. I can hardly keep track of who's pals with whom and who's planning to murder whom! Talk about living in interesting times!

7th January 1480

I've been following this really weird-looking old chap all day today. He had the most incredible face I've ever seen. Huge chin, massive nose and really big staring eyes. I just couldn't stop looking at him and I tailed him for hours, making notes in my head so I could draw him when I got home. And here he is!

That's the thing about so-called ugly faces, more often than not, they're the most interesting ones.

Learning with Leo

Drawing faces: Look at the features of lots of folks' phizogs.

CRIPES! LOOK AT THE EYES ON THAT ONE! ... AND THE GNASHERS ON HIM!

Memorize all their different-shaped heads, mouths, eyes, necks, chins, etc. Do a hooter survey, just like I did!

LEONARDO'S AWESOME HOOTERS AND STUNNING SCHNOZZLES. WHICH ONE'S YOURS?

The faces of people sitting in dark doorways make superb subjects for pictures. The bright light coming from outside and the deep darkness inside make a brilliant contrast, which throws their features into sharp relief – this makes them stand out really well and often adds great beauty to their faces.

Leo made his survey of noses, mouths, chins and whatnot in one of his notebooks. In addition to the gillion-megabyte memory hard disk that was his super-brain, those notebooks became a huge database full of brilliant drawings, astonishing ideas and his most awesome observations, not to mention dozens and dozens of dazzling inventions. He once said:

From the dawn of the day the air is filled with masses of images and they're all like magnets to my eyes.

And he just couldn't stop gawping at each and every one of them as he frantically stashed them in his huge and infinitely powerful memory.

MAMMA MIA! CHECK OUT THAT WOMAN'S AMAZING CONK!

SHEESH! LOOK AT THAT CAT'S WEIRD TAIL, AND THE WAY THAT HORSE'S MUSCLES...

Makes you think, doesn't it? And even more astonishingly:

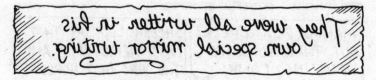

All will be explained ... but only if you read the next chapter...

HAVE NOTEBOOK, WILL SCRIBBLE...

Leonardo is generally thought to have really got going on his notebooks when he was about 30 and, with his super-brain frenziedly flitting from one idea to another, he spent the rest of his life covering page after page with sketches of people, animals and plants, diagrams for machines and weapons, designs for musical instruments, lists of books ... all sorts of things ... even shopping lists. For example, in one notebook, there are some really complicated jottings about canals and geometry, followed by the words:

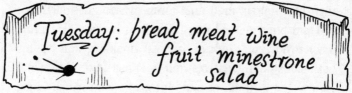

Tuesday: bread meat wine fruit minestrone salad

As a result of all his non-stop scribbling, Leonardo ended up with a staggering *13,000* pages of notes and drawings on almost every subject under the sun. Which is probably why he was always short of paper! He'd probably have given his right arm for a computer.

One of the things Leonardo liked to do best before he went to sleep was to lie in the dark and imagine all the different contours of the interesting stuff he'd seen during the day.

In his notebooks he said that he recommended doing this as it was really useful for imprinting things on the memory (and definitely beats counting sheep).

Write confusing

The amazing thing is Leonardo wrote almost all of his notes back-to-front and inside-out ... well, sort of. Important: To read this next bit you're going to need a mirror (or a remarkably agile brain).

He was what is known as ambidextrous, in other words he was able to write with both his left and right hand. He seemed to prefer using his left hand but this caused him problems because in those days biros were few and far between (i.e. non-existent) and people used pens, which they constantly had to dip in a pot of ink. If you wrote from left to right with one of these your left hand trailed in the ink, smudging your work and giving you a permanent stain just below your little finger.

Brain befuddled? Take Codex!

A few years after he died, Leonardo's precious notebooks and other various bits and pieces of paper he'd written his amazing ideas on began to disappear. Some were sold off, some were simply lost through carelessness, while others were pinched by souvenir hunters. Over the centuries that followed about 6,000 pages of notes vanished entirely, but fortunately the other 7,000 or so were collected together in volumes.

Each volume is known as a codex, which, despite sounding like a fast-acting flu remedy, simply means big wadge of written or typed pages. These codices have now ended up in museums and libraries around the world and are normally named after the person or organization who last owned them. For example, the *Codex Arundel* is named after Lord Arundel who was a keen British collector of Leonardoabilia. However, the *Codex Atlanticus* is named after the really big sheets of paper, normally used in atlases, that Leonardo wrote that particular set of notes on.

In 1994, the mega-rich computer whizz-kid Bill Gates paid $30 million for Leonardo's *Codex Leicester* and not long afterwards he got his micro-nerds to turn the whole caboodle into digital code so that it could be read and marvelled at

clearly and easily on CD-ROM. Bill said that Leonardo had been one of his heroes since childhood and that notebooks like the *Codex Leicester* were 'hundreds of years ahead of their time' because they were full of notes about really modern gizmos such as submarines and helicopters (but not 560 gigabyte PCs).

It's not just Bill Gates who's noticed Leo's knack of being streets ahead of the thinking of his day and age. Someone else once said that Leonardo was: 'like a man who woke too early while everyone else was asleep.' In other words, they were saying that his doodles had anticipated the astonishing machines that would be created in the age of technology which only really got going some three centuries after his death. Hundreds and hundreds of pages in his notebooks are covered in

notes and designs for all kinds of devices, many of which were finally realized when latter-day boffins and big-brains got to grips with some of the practical problems that had prevented Leonardo turning his dreams into reality.

Leonardo's gizmos for leisurely lifestyles

Not all of Leonardo's ideas were entirely original. Sometimes he took ideas that other inventors had dreamed up, then improved on them. However, his output of awesome and original ideas is quite astonishing. A lot of his inventions were weapons of war and you can read about them on page 133 (you blood-thirsty little ghoul, you), but he also designed friendly devices that were intended to make everyone's lives much *less* painful and far *more* pleasant.

Blood, sweat and gears

Leonardo was fascinated by cunning mechanical devices such as pulleys, winches, ratchets, levers and gears and was forever thinking up new ways in which they could be incorporated into labour-saving machines.

To spare honest, horny-handed, working chaps their aching backs and blisters he doodled this double digging and drilling machine. Instead of having to spend hours digging dirty great holes in the ground with a spade, this machine was intended to whirl and thrust its way deep down into the soil in no time at all. The idea was

that a couple of men would rotate the top bar and the huge drill would bite into the earth like a super-powered mechanical mole. Once it had drilled as deep as was necessary, the men would rotate the second bar in the opposite direction and all the earth would be lifted out of the hole.

The car in front is a Leonardo

When it came to creating cool wheels Leonardo really was ahead of his time. He's thought to have drawn his design for a self-moving car in 1478. Nevertheless, despite his efforts to make all the Renaissance world's horses unemployed, it was going to be another 400 years before fully functioning automobiles would begin polluting the atmosphere and generally causing worldwide gridlock.

Leonardo's car design was actually of the non-polluting variety because his idea was that his *machina* (Italian for 'car') would get its power from a batch of springs that slowly released their energy, rather like the way a spring on a clockwork toy train works. The power from the car's leaf springs was transmitted to its wheels through a series of gear wheels.

Leo also designed a water-powered alarm clock, an automatic roasting spit, a self-closing door, a paper feeder for a printing press, a metal screw maker, an air cooling system and a magnifying projector. And here are designs for a few more inventions he also thought up earlier than everyone else:

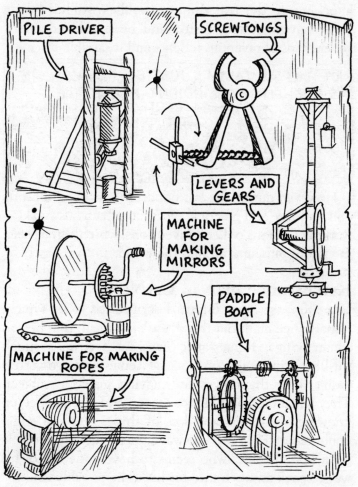

It's not known whether Leo actually got round to making three-dimensional working versions of his inventions. It's possible he was so full of new ideas that he'd be off sketching a fresh one before he had found time to make a working version of the one he'd just thought of. And anyway, if he did ever get round to knocking up the real things, they'll probably be long gone, having rotted, rusted and been gobbled up by generations of ravenous rodents and insatiable insects.

However, during the last hundred years or so, all sorts of inquisitive and practical types have been busy making working versions of Leo's inventions, which can be seen in various museums around the world.

Renaissance man ... CAN!

Leonardo is now often described as the typical Renaissance man. But this doesn't *just* mean that he was a man living in Renaissance times. As there was so much thrilling stuff going on, lots of Renaissance go-getters didn't limit themselves to studying just one subject. They had a bash at all kinds of stuff and often ended up knowing about lots and lots of things. As you've no doubt realized by now, Leo was a phenomenally versatile genius-of-all-trades who seems to have gone out of his way to pack as much into his life as he possibly could.

This multi-skilling way of embracing learning and knowledge is quite unlike the modern approach, where people specialize in the study of just one or two subjects. As a result, the phrase 'Renaissance man' is now used to describe people who are knowledgeable in many areas. The modern Renaissance person might be someone who knows lots and lots about arty subjects, but can talk the hind legs off a laboratory rat when it comes to matters scientific (and can probably play the tuba whilst painting a masterpiece, tuning a sports-car engine, writing a novel and cooking a gourmet dinner for six).

It's most people's opinion that the phenomenally talented Leonardo more or less out-Renaissanced just about all his mates and contemporaries. His amazing versatility and all-round brilliance were certainly going to come in useful when he decided to up sticks and try and land a top job in macho Milan...

CIAO, BIG NOB! GIZZA JOB!

In 1482, when he was about 30 years old, Leonardo left Florence and went to Milan. No one's quite sure why. Some say it's because the Medici wanted to get together with the Sforzas, the rulers of Milan, in the hope that they'd help them in their struggles against their enemies, and Lorenzo the Magnificent had decided that sending Duke Ludovico their brightest talent would gain their favour. It's more likely that it was simply because Leonardo had decided that shifting to Milan would be a really smart career move.

> **Leonardo's Lost Notebook 1482**
> Have just arrived in Milan. It's absolutely massive! At least three times bigger than Florence. And talk about security conscious. There are armed men everywhere! The city gates are guarded by huge towers. And a vast moat with a portcullis and drawbridge!

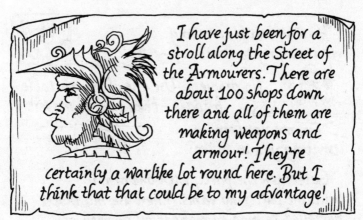

I have just been for a stroll along the Street of the Armourers. There are about 100 shops down there and all of them are making weapons and armour! They're certainly a warlike lot round here. But I think that that could be to my advantage!

Although Milan was a much bigger and busier place than Florence, it wasn't exactly teeming with great painters, craftsmen and sculptors. Going there was really just the break Leonardo was looking for. And, not being one to hide his light under a bushel, he took the opportunity to write himself a reference letter, telling Duke Ludovico what an all-round talented and brilliant sort of bloke he was. This is more or less what it said:

Dear Duke of Milan,

Buongiorno! I hear you fancy becoming ruler of all Italy. Well, your Dukeness, for that you're going to need dozens of devices for death and destruction! And I'm the man to dream them up! Leonardo da Vinci is my name and I'm devilishly good at devising gizmos to flatten foes! Just consider these...

81

Leo's no-nonsense Nativity

Talk about not underestimating your own abilities! Surprisingly (or not), Leo didn't hear back from Duke Ludovico straight away, but he hung around Milan in the hope that sooner or later he would.

As things turned out, his first big art job didn't come from the Duke but from some Franciscan friars who asked him to paint a picture, which is now known as the *Virgin of the Rocks*. In the contract for the work, the friars stated that the oil painting was to show: Mary on a throne alongside Jesus, perched on a golden platform; a couple of prophets; God, dressed in blue and gold, gazing down at them (and no doubt looking chuffed to pieces); two angels (what's a religious painting without a few angels flitting around?); and everyone wearing a halo! In other words, it was to be very traditional sort of religious painting.

However, when the job was finished, the friars got a bit of a shock! Not only had Leonardo left out God, the prophets, one of the angels, the throne *and* the halos, he'd also painted baby Jesus with no clothes on and sitting on the grass (it's a wonder he didn't give him a romper suit and a teething ring).

The friars should have known better really. No one gets to be the most famous figure of the Renaissance era without breaking a few thousand rules along the way.

Although the friars weren't too keen on it, the picture created a sensation in Milan and, what with his general all-round cleverness and growing fame, Leonardo was finally noticed by Duke Ludovico, who then became his patron (that is, he regularly began giving him money to paint things and make things for him).

Ludovico Sforza (1452–1508)

Leonardo's new boss, Ludovico, was the ruler of the Duchy of Milan and was nicknamed 'The Moor' because

he had a dark complexion. He shouldn't really have been ruler because his nephew, Gian Galeazzo, was the rightful duke. However, because Gian Galeazzo was still quite young, Ludovico decided to do the job for him. Then, in 1494, as bad luck (and Uncle Ludo) would have it, Gian Galeazzo died suddenly in somewhat mysterious circumstances, leaving Ludovico in charge.

Duke Ludovico was a great believer in predicting his future by the stars and consequently employed large numbers of astrologers to tell him what lay around the next corner. He was also a great believer in *protecting* his future and employed huge numbers of soldiers, spies and assassins to look after him, not to mention lots of armourers and military engineers. Ludovico and his immediate ancestors were a warlike lot who had got where they were by adopting a punch-first-ask-questions-afterwards approach to politics. For instance, Ludovico's grandad passed down this useful advice to his descendants:

Never hit your servant or your companion. But, if you do ... finish them off quick!

EEK!

Multi-tasking in Milan

Realizing that Renaissance Italy was now getting a worldwide reputation for being arty and sophisticated and progressive, Ludovico decided that he'd like to become a bit more like his more-cultured neighbours, the Medici, so having a man of Leonardo's talents at his beck and call was just the ticket. In fact, when he put his mind to it, Ludo just couldn't stop thinking of ways to keep his new in-castle-creative-consultant rushed off his feet. Leonardo didn't have just one job at Ludo's palace – he had loads!

SO, MASTER, WHAT WOULD YOU LIKE CREATING TODAY? YOUR WISHES ARE OUR COMMANDS

These are three of the main duties he was expected to perform:

1 Court painter

Leonardo's job was to paint flattering portraits of Ludo's chums and rellies. One of the pictures he did was this painting of Ludovico's 17-year-old girlfriend, Cecilia Gallerani, which is now known as the *Lady with an ermine*.

It's said that Leonardo got Cecilia to hold the ermine because the Greek word for ermine is galê, and that sounds a bit like her name (good job she wasn't called Cecilia Stinkbug then).

2 Master of the court's festivities

This meant that Leonardo was in charge of planning plays and musical performances, designing sets and costumes and generally making sure that everyone had a good time at the various knees-ups held by Duke Ludo. When Ludovico's nephew, Gian Galeazzo, got married to the King of Naples's granddaughter, Ludo decided that he'd quite like to give him a wedding bash with an astrological theme, so Leonardo organized a real astral extravaganza involving all manner of gadgets and gizmos. After the Duke and his mates had boozed and banqueted for a while they wandered along to his theatre to see what Leonardo had prepared for them. They weren't disappointed. As music played, the curtains were dropped to reveal a range of mountains on the stage. The stage then began to revolve and the mountains opened up. Inside was a glittering dome that looked just like a starry sky. Arranged around the sky were actors dressed as the seven planets who all revolved gracefully while other actors stepped forward to make speeches praising the bride.

3 General engineer and master of works

These were busy times in the Duchy of Milan. New transport projects were being started, buildings were being erected and preparations were constantly being made in case war should break out. Leonardo had to supervise the construction of canals, knock up architectural drawings for additions to the new cathedral and oversee the pouring of molten lead into moulds for cannonballs.

But it wasn't just Duke Ludo's demands that got Leo's creative juices flowing. He hadn't been in Milan all that long when events set him thinking of even bigger and bolder projects!

THE MILAN MESSENGER
Spring 1485

BLACK DEATH DOWNS DOZENS

The plague is back! Our citizens are going down like flies. And what with our gravediggers being so greedy (they really do charge the earth), there are rotting bodies all over the show as rellies just can't afford to get their loved ones properly buried! Quite sensibly, our wise and noble ruler, Duke Ludo, has hopped it to his house in the hills.

If you are unlucky enough to have a loved one catch the plague, all the usual precautions apply: keep them well out of other people's way, burn their clothes and blankets, and pray for the best! Let's hope this is nothing more than a minor outbreak and that it will have passed away in a week or two.

Leonardo's Lost Notebook 1485

A terrible disaster has struck Milan. Tens of thousands of people are dead from plague. It's impossible to walk five metres without stumbling across some poor wretch who has fallen victim to it.

> *There are dead and dying everywhere.*
> *But it's no wonder we've ended up in this mess. The people in this stinking city are more overcrowded than goats in their pen on market day, there's filth absolutely everywhere and the very air we breathe reeks to high heaven of death and disease! What Milan needs is a huge once-and-for-all makeover job. And I'm the chap to do it!*

Leo's super-city

Leo let his super-brain and awesome architectural imagination loose on the problem of Milan's terrible overcrowding and health problems. He came up with all sorts of designs and models...

He finally decided that the only solution was to rebuild the entire city at the edge of the river. To give a feeling of order and spaciousness, the new city would be spread over a much larger area than the old one and divided into ten separate towns. Canals would criss-cross the whole area so that people could water their gardens from them and travel from place to place in boats (and perhaps even swim to work on really sunny days). Set at intervals along the canals would be locks with huge paddle wheels that would enable the Milanese to keep their streets clean and fresh by giving them regular slooshings with canal water.

Leo's marvellous city would be built on two levels. The upper level would be home to toffs (Leo, the Duke and his pals) and beneath that would be a lower level for all the shops and traders and common folk. To encourage general cleanliness and hygiene, all the public buildings in this new super-city would have spiral staircases. Why? To stop mucky folk dumping their rubbish and taking crafty tiddles in the dark corners as they were so fond of doing in the square-shaped ones.

And finally, for the convenience and well-being of everyone, there would be public loos absolutely everywhere, all based on Leo's own personal design.

THE LEO LOO

LOTS OF HOLES IN THE CEILING... TO LET OUT THE PONG, OF COURSE!

SEAT THAT SWIVELS BACK INTO PLACE ALL ON ITS OWN

Top and bottom of it all

Some people might think it was a bit unkind of Leo to see ordinary folk as not being worthy of an above-stairs existence in his ideal city. However, like almost everyone in his day, he generally thought that people were either born to be bright-as-buttons-movers-and-shakers or dull-as-ditchwater-plodders, and should know their place in society. In fact, once, when he was writing about ordinary people, he said:

> *During their entire lives many of them contribute nothing to the world other than the waste products of their bodies.*

(But he didn't put it half as politely as that.)

91

Leonardo never did get to see his design for a super-city turned into bricks and mortar. The plague eventually subsided and the survivors simply continued with their familiar filthy habits. But perhaps Leo wasn't too bothered about creating his hugely hygienic hyper-town at this point. By now his super-brain was no doubt distracted by thoughts of mounting his next big project! And this really was a very **BIG** project indeed!

LEONARDO'S
HUMONGOUS GREAT HORSE

No matter how famous individuals are in their lifetime, they often get forgotten after they're dead unless people have something to remember them by. Painters, boffins and musicians leave their pictures, inventions and tunes behind them, but politicians and warriors often don't leave anything apart from pillaged villages, shattered cities and broken promises. In order to make sure his dad, Francesco, was remembered for all time (not to mention giving the Milanese pigeons somewhere interesting to perch), Ludovico Sforza wanted someone to create a really massive bronze model of his old dad riding a humongous great horse. The horse alone was going to be a staggering seven metres high (almost as tall as two double-decker buses, one on top of the other), and was going to be the biggest cast sculpture ever created.

MONUMENT IDEAS
Enormous elk X
Massive moose X
Large lemur X
Big badger
Humungous

How to make your own bronze sculpture

Make a magnificent bronze sculpture of your favourite horse/hamster/boyfriend/girlfriend/TV personality in the style of the great Renaissance sculptors and bronze casters.

You will need:

An anvil, a few tons of bronze, lots of plaster, a blacksmith's forge, half a dozen skilled helpers (preferably fifteenth-century Renaissance craftsmen), some modelling clay, a huge oven, lots of wax (ear-hole sort will not do), hammer and chisel, saw, masses of bendy metal, a large furnace, protective clothing, a really good life insurance policy, a big strong winch.

What to do:

1 Make a clay model over a metal framework of your subject in the pose you want it to be.

2 Cover the clay model in wax.

3 Bung some sticky-out wax tubes on your model. Don't ask why! Just do as you're told!

4 Using wet plaster, build a mould round your wax model. The wax tubes should poke through the plaster when it hardens. Hold the blocks in place with strong iron bands that you have forged on the anvil.

5 Heat up the plaster mould in a dirty great oven so that all the wax melts. Now, here's the clever bit! Those wax tubes will melt, creating outlet ducts that allow the rest of wax to run out. See!

6 You've now got a plaster mould with a hollow middle that's the exact shape of your model.

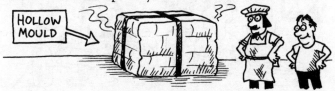

7 Dig a dirty great hole, then, using your big strong winch to lift the mould, bury it in the hole.

8 Heat up the bronze in your furnace. When it's so hot it's glowing whitish-yellow and really, really runny, pour it into a hole at the top of your mould.

Warning! Molten bronze is really dangerous. If there's a change in the weather or temperature, or any dampness has got inside your mould, there's a good chance the whole thing will explode, showering you and your helpers with white hot metal. (That's partly why you've buried the mould.)

9 Go down the tavern with your helpers for some wine, cheese and olives. Stay there until you think the whole thing has cooled off.

10 Return to your workshop and haul your mould out of the hole with your winch, then break off all the plaster blocks with your hammer and chisel.

11 You should now have a lovely bronze replica of your model. Saw off the sticky-out duct tubes and trim away any other grotty bits.

12 Now give your masterwork a) a good polish; b) some decorative engraved twiddly bits; or c) to the bin-men.

Leonardo was the perfect person for the task of creating the giant gee-gee, as he was a huge horse fan. And, being so rich and powerful, Duke Ludo had stables full of super-horses (just like modern billionaires have garages full of super-cars) for Leo to study. In preparation for the creation of the huge horse Leo set about sketching them, measuring them, and making records of the different ways they walked, trotted, galloped (and rolled on their backs and asked for their tummies to be tickled). He even dissected horses so he could find out just how they worked and exactly how all their various bits and pieces were joined together.

Eventually he'd got together enough sketches and notes to actually begin work on the colossal clay model that would be the basis for the mould into which the bronze would be poured. After ten years (on and off), of squidging, pummelling and smoothing, the clay model was finished. In 1493 Leonardo put it on display in the courtyard of the Castello Sforzesco (Sforza Castle) so that the stunned citizens of Milan could gaze at the wondrous beast and say things like:

And then, in 1494, just when it looked like the dream of the wondrous gigantic gee-gee would finally become a reality, the French invaded Italy. Realizing he would need to defend his Duchy, Duke Ludo used all the city's bronze to make cannons, so plans for the final statue were shelved! The giant clay model was just left where it stood until, in the second France vs Milan war in five years, the victorious French finally entered Milan in 1499 and their archers decided to use it for target practice.

Tail note

Horse-Kong finally did get made. But not by Leonardo. When it finally saw the light of day he'd been dead for nearly 500 years. During the 1970s, a rich American art enthusiast heard the story of the massive horse and decided to pay for some artists to create not just one, but two, full-size bronze replicas. And, using the centuries old modelling and bronze casting technique described above, they did just that. One of the giant horses was sent to Milan in the 1990s as a tribute to Leonardo's genius and the general wonderfulness of Renaissance Italy, while the other was put in a sculpture park in Michigan, USA.

Leonardo's Lost Notebook 1489-1490

1489

Busy as ever! Quite excited at the moment because; a) a French chap I met has promised to tell me just how big the sun is...

and b) an astronomy essay by Aristotle, the great Greek philosopher, has just been translated into Italian. Can't wait to read it! I'm also working on some rather interesting design ideas at the moment, including:
a crane for emptying ditches

a table lamp with adjustable brightness

AHH!

and this armchair that takes away the aches and pains of whoever sits in it.

Things-to-do-list for this week

1) Measure Castle Sforza (as soon as I get a spare moment).
2) Find out how to make a cannon.
3) Ask Signor Portinari how people in Flanders manage to run on the ice.
4) Find out how to build dams on rivers and how much they cost.
5) Buy some more minestrone. (yum yum!)

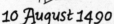

12 July 1490
I've got myself a new servant. He's ten years old, has black curly hair and his name is Giacomo. Found him living on the streets and dressed in rags.

10 August 1490
Little Giacomo is proving to be a nuisance! Got my tailor to make him some new clothes but now the little so-and-so has stolen the money I put out to pay for them! He denies it of course, but I know it's him. I've decided to rename him Salai, which means 'little devil'!

18 September 1490

Last week we were busy preparing for a huge tournament to be held in fancy-dress costumes designed by me. While the grooms were trying on their savages' outfits, Salai stole one of their purses. That boy is driving me crazy!

Leonardo's lifestyle

As you'd expect with such a special and unique human being, Leo had strong views and opinions on just about every subject going. And, of course, his attitudes and tastes had a big influence on the way he organized his life and related to his fellow human beings (not to mention his fellow furry beasts and feathery friends).

Family life

Leonardo never got married, nor did he have any children of his own, because he preferred to spend his time with chaps. From the age of 39, he did have the company of little Salai (who later became somewhat-bigger Salai). And, despite the fact that the lad was such a scallywag and forever up to mischief, Leonardo spoiled him rotten, giving him nice food, dressing him in posh clothes and generally making a fuss of him. It's reported that he attempted to teach Salai to paint but the lad turned out to be rubbish at art so Leonardo employed him to run errands instead. About 20 years after he first came to live with Leonardo, Salai was still driving his boss nuts with his bad behaviour. However, rather than throwing him out, Leonardo simply said to him:

> Salai, I want to make peace. No more war. I give in!

All creatures great and small

Leo had always been fascinated by animals and eventually became a sort of early animal liberationist and vegetarian. In order to carry out his good deeds he would go to the local market where there were always cages full of wild birds for sale. In those days people liked to have wild songbirds in cages by their front door because they sang so attractively (and they were much prettier than Rottweilers). Leo would often buy whole cages full of these wild birds (but only if they were going cheep), then immediately set them free.

SAME AGAIN NEXT WEEK, MR DA VINCI?

He also decided it was wrong for animals to suffer just so that humans could pig out on pork chops and be gluttons for mutton (but only if it was going sheep) so he became a vegetarian, much preferring to eat things like salad, mushrooms and his beloved minestrone.

Those pesky priests

It's not surprising that Leonardo threw the water on the priest. He just wasn't a big fan of the churchy-chaps of his day. This is more or less what he said about them:

> *They talk too much and they get paid too much. They laze around in palaces because they say that pleases God no end. What's even worse, they trick poor people into putting up with their terrible lives here on Earth by promising them that one day they'll go to Paradise and live happily ever after.*

But, considering the sort of things the fifteenth-century Popes and their pals got up to, like forgiving people their sins if they paid money to the Church, it wasn't in the least bit surprising that Leonardo said this!

Leo might have thought that the clergy could be a pain at times but he frequently had to rely on them to pay his bills. That giant horse wasn't the only really big project he was engaged in during his time in Milan. In order to earn the money to put food on his table he was also busy painting a huge picture of someone else's very important dinner date...

JESUS CHRIST...SUPPER-STAR

The *Last Supper* is the only painting by Leonardo that's still in the exact spot he painted it. Which is not surprising, as he painted it straight on to the wall of a refectory (dining hall) in the monastery of Santa Maria delle Grazie in Milan. Duke Ludovico had recommended Leo to the monks and had been nagging him to paint the *Last Supper* mural (wall painting) for some time. He eventually began working on it around 1495. It's a very appropriate picture for a refectory as it shows Jesus and his disciples having their last meal together before he is crucified (with Jesus about to tell them that one of them would soon betray him).

The painting, which has been described as the most beautiful picture in the world, is a whopping great 4.6 metres high and 8.8 metres long. It's also 2 metres above the floor. Leonardo had some scaffolding constructed so he could work up close to his subject. One of the many brilliant things about the *Last Supper* is the way Leonardo cleverly uses perspective to draw the viewer's eye into the picture and focus on Jesus' face, despite the fact that the whole painting is two metres above their eye level.

When Leonardo got going on a new project he really threw himself into it wholeheartedly. Here's what one person who witnessed the great man painting the *Last Supper* more or less said about Leonardo's approach to his work:

He gets here really early in the morning then climbs on to his scaffolding and immediately gets painting. Sometimes he's up there from sunrise until sunset, never putting down his brush, forgetting to eat and drink, and painting without stopping for even a second! On the other hand, sometimes he comes here for three or four days but never touches the painting. He just spends hours in front of it with his arms folded ... staring and thinking! Once, in the middle of the day, when the sun was at its hottest, he turned up here from Corte Vecchia (where he's doing that massive clay horse) climbed up the scaffold, grabbed his brush, slapped on a couple of dabs of paint, then clambered down again and disappeared!

An impressive attitude! But then, after a time, problems occurred, which interfered with Leonardo's progress…

Leonardo's Lost Notebook 1497–1498

1497

Last Supper going well. Despite the moaning monks! I've already finished eleven of the apostles, only Judas to do now. Have done his body but can't find a suitably wicked-looking model for the sneaky traitor's ugly mush!

1497 (a few months later)

Still trying to find face for Judas. And the monks are moaning again! The head monk, the Prior, has been to Duke Ludovico, he wants to know just <u>when</u> I'll be finished and has complained about my painting gear cluttering up his precious dining-room. When Ludovico mentioned this to me I told him not a day goes by when I don't work two hours on the picture.

1498

The Prior has been to Ludo again and said not only has a whole year gone by without me touching the painting but I've only been to see it once. Which is true! But I told Ludo I worked on it two hours every day as usual. Which puzzled him! So I had to explain to him that even when us artists <u>appear</u> not to be working, we are still as busy as ever… in our heads! And in my search for a suitably wicked-looking model for the face of Judas, I've been wandering around the dodgy part of the city, where all the thugs and thieves hang out, checking out their mean-looking mugs. I told Ludo that if I couldn't find a suitably evil-looking git to use for Judas, I'd use the Prior's face. Talk about laugh… his Excellency almost burst his britches!

1498 (a few months later)

Have finally found the villain and finished Judas's face. So… the Last Supper is now finished. Done and dusted! Once and for all!

Well, that's what Leonardo thought! But things didn't quite work out the way he'd intended.

A good meal ruined

Most Italian Renaissance artists created murals by using the fresco technique, which involves slapping water-based paint onto areas of fresh plaster. This is a painting technique that requires careful planning and then a decisive attitude with no dithering because...

This wasn't Leonardo's style at all – he liked to fiddle with his figures, sometimes repainting them several times, whilst regularly stopping to have little thinks about what he was doing. In view of this he decided to create the fresco by applying very thick tempera paint to a double layer of plaster. However, for some reason he didn't bother to *test* this new approach before using it on his huge work of art. And to make matters worse, it's thought that the wall was suffering from rising damp.

So, after three years of planning, hard slog, and putting up with moaning monks, the most beautiful painting in the world began to disintegrate before everyone's eyes!

But that wasn't all. A whole series of other disasters proceeded to befall the painting, including attempts by various well-meaning bodge-up artists to try to put things right!

The Last Supper: a tragic timeline

1499 Damp and dust begin to damage the picture almost as soon as Leonardo's finished it.

1500 Flood water fills the refectory. Moisture creeps up the wall and the rot sets in.

1503 Paint begins flaking off the *Last Supper* faster than leaves fall from oak trees in autumn.

OH, BROTHER ANTONIO, YOU REALLY WILL HAVE TO DO SOMETHING ABOUT YOUR DANDRUFF!

1556 The *Last Supper* has now deteriorated so much that it's described as nothing more than a dazzling stain and a mass of blobs.

1624 A hole is cut in the wall to create a doorway leading to the monastery kitchen. It's just where Jesus' tootsies and the tablecloth are. It's later blocked up again but you can see the join! And Jesus' feet don't reappear!

1700s Two attempts are made to restore sections of the picture but the restorers do more harm than good when they pull off huge chunks of the picture and repaint them in their own style.

1796 During their conquest of Italy, Napoleon's troops store their horses' fodder in the refectory (even though Napoleon told them not to). The men are also said to have passed their time by throwing bricks at the heads of the apostles.

1800 The refectory is flooded again.

1820–1908 Three more attempts are made to patch up the picture.

1943 A Second World War bomb falls on the refectory roof but the *Last Supper* escapes damage, protected by a wall of sandbags.

The multi-million lira makeover!

In 1977, the Italian government paid a group of art experts to do a makeover on the *Last Supper* and restore it to its former glory once and for all. The restorers set about carefully scraping away all the paint and glue of the previous patch-up jobs. And then, millimetre by millimetre, flake by flake, and tiny brushstroke by tiny brushstroke, what was left of the original picture began to reappear! A mere *20 years* later, the experts were finished! Yes! It took them almost ten times as long to restore the *Last Supper* as it took Leonardo to paint it! It's now on show, but only for 15 minutes at a time, and to groups of no more than 25 people (who must hold their breath the whole time they're admiring it). Special dust-absorbing carpets and dust-filtering pipes have been installed so that the air remains free of the crud and gunge that ruined the painting in the first place. However, some art experts say that so much fiddling has been done with the 500-year-old picture that it's no longer a genuine Leonardo (more of a Leonar*didn't*).

How to paint a magnificent masterpiece in the style of Leonardo da Vinci

You will need: a palette, paintbrushes, paper, pencils, charcoal or black pastel, oil paints, linseed oil, a wall or a big wooden panel, a sharp pin, cleaning rags, long white beard (optional, but really useful for wiping your paintbrushes on), and some inspiration.

What to do:

1 Make some preliminary sketches and studies of the things that are going to be in your painting. Continue doing this until you feel you know your subject well.

2 Combine all your ideas into a small composition. Copy your composition on to big sheets of paper in the form of a larger cartoon the same size as you want your final

masterpiece to be. Leonardo often used to glue lots of sheets of paper together for this as wall-sized drawing books were quite hard to come by (and still are).

3 Attach your cartoon to the wooden panel or wall, then, using your pin or another sharp instrument, make little holes along the outline of your drawing.

4 Rub charcoal dust over the pinholes so that it goes through them on to your wall or panel.

5 Remove your cartoon. You should now have your masterpiece outlined in lots of little black dots. (Don't bother joining the dots.)

6 If you are painting on a panel, using a neutral, earthy colour, like brown, start your underpainting. This is the old-fashioned oil-painting method whereby you fill in the main shapes in your picture and model them (make them look 3-D) by using darker tones for the shadowy bits and paler tones for the lighter bits.

7 When your brown underpainting is dry you can begin to colour it by adding glazes. Glazes are thin, semi-transparent washes of colour diluted with linseed oil. Fifteenth-century artists would paint layer after layer of these glazes creating beautiful, glowing colours.

8 Put in the highlights (bright, sparkly bits where the light catches objects) of your picture by using white paint or a colour mixed with white.

9 Stand back and admire your masterpiece, but whatever you do don't give it a title!
10 And don't sign it.

Top tips: While you're working, don't get too bogged down in technique and remember to allow your creative genius to run free (but please ... keep it away from busy main roads).

While you are waiting for your underpainting and glazes to dry do something futuristic, useful and Leonardo-like by going off and inventing a time machine or a car engine that runs on water.

Leonardo's Lost Notebook 1499

Early spring 1499
Well, I've got a great life here in Milan. All very satisfying. I've got a good bit of money saved up and done some great work, investigations and experiments. And, what's more, his Ludoness has given me a nice little vineyard just outside town. I'm thinking of building a house on it. Just one little worry, though. I've heard tell King Louis XII of France is cosying up to the Doge in Venice. This could mean trouble for Duke Ludo.

Early summer 1499

Been carrying out some very interesting experiments to do with movement and weight. Also busy knocking together a snazzy little heater to warm up the Duchess of Aragon's bath water. I think three parts hot to one part cold is about the right mix for the perfect soak.

THE MILAN MESSENGER

June 1499

WAR!

IT'S OFFICIAL! We are at war with France. King Louis and his army have crossed the Alps and are capturing forts and citadels on the western edges of our Duchy of Milan.

And in the meantime the Venetians are attacking us from the east!

Nevertheless, we must put up a brave resistance to these foreign invaders.

THE MILAN MESSENGER
August 1499

MORE FRENCH VICTORIES!

As the victorious French army continues its relentless advance on our city we are now getting reports of crowd disturbances here in Milan itself. Duke Ludovico has been trying to get the crowds behind him but with no luck.

STOP PRESS: An enraged mob has just hanged the city treasurer! And all our generals have gone and run away. Shame on them!

By October 1499, King Louis XII and his army had marched into Milan. Duke Ludovico scarpered, and widespread looting and killing broke out around the city.

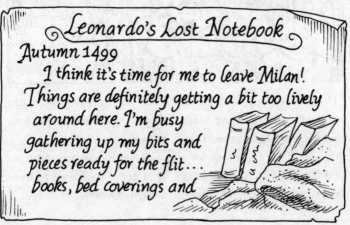

Leonardo's Lost Notebook

Autumn 1499

I think it's time for me to leave Milan! Things are definitely getting a bit too lively around here. I'm busy gathering up my bits and pieces ready for the flit... books, bed coverings and suchlike. Must collect that little stove from St Mary's, the one I used when I was painting the Last Supper. I'll sell everything I can't carry. And send my savings to Florence. You can't be too careful! Now, things to buy: tablecloth and towels; a hat; shoes; four pairs of tights; a big goatskin coat; some leather to make more coats; paper; box of colours; maybe some watermelon and lily seeds too?

WATER, WATER, EVERYWHERE!

And that was that! In 1500, after 17 years in Milan, Leonardo went on the road. And, on and off, he was going to be on the road for almost the rest of his life; moving back and forth between Florence, Milan, Rome and one or two other Italian cities, staying a year or so here, a few months there, and constantly being at the beck-and-call of whichever big banana happened to be ruling the roost.

The first place he settled was Venice. Once there, he began advising the Venetians on how to splat the Turks, who were busy menacing Venice at the request of Duke Ludovico. It didn't bother Leonardo that the Venetians were partly responsible for downing Ludovico. People weren't like that in sixteenth-century Italy. The only way you survived was to be loyal to the biggest bully in the playground! Not nice ... but a fact of life!

Leonardo makes a big splash

At many times during his life Leonardo had water on the brain. His amazing mind was awash with ideas about the

120

stuff. He said, 'The world needs water like our bodies need blood.' However, when he was a young man, whopping great floods had devastated his home area on several occasions and he was very aware of water's terrible destructive powers. He said that what terrified him more than earthquakes or volcanoes was the sight of a river bursting its banks, then washing away and drowning all that stood in its path: adults, children, horses, cattle, trees, pigs and houses.

He worked out that, over vast periods of time, water slowly wears away rocks in the process known as erosion, that valleys are carved out of the earth by rivers and that sometimes seas recede to reveal dirty great mountain ranges.

Leonardo's Lost Notebook

May 1500

I've been puzzling over how all those old shells came to be on top of a big mountain near here. Local people think they just grew there, in the rocks. Which is obviously <u>nonsense!</u> Others think they got washed all the way up there in the Flood that's in the Bible. Which is also <u>nonsense!</u> No! What I'm beginning to think is that those mountain tops might once have been sea beds. And the shells belonged to all the sea creatures that died and sank into the mud.

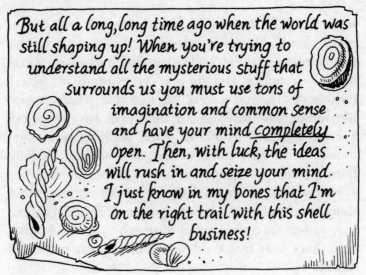

But all a long, long time ago when the world was still shaping up! When you're trying to understand all the mysterious stuff that surrounds us you must use tons of imagination and common sense and have your mind _completely_ open. Then, with luck, the ideas will rush in and seize your mind. I just know in my bones that I'm on the right trail with this shell business!

People forgot all about Leonardo's thoughts about rocks and fossils for about 300 years. Then some bright spark geologist type decided to research the great man's ideas a bit more and discovered that he'd been right all along.

Leo's super-brainwaves

As a result of being so completely fascinated by the wet stuff, Leo was forever dreaming up schemes to harness the phenomenal power of water. Like these...

Super-brainwave one: Devious dam

During the 1490s, when Florence was at war with nearby Pisa, Leonardo thought up a scheme to take away the city of Pisa's water supply and dry up the harbour by diverting the River Arno. His idea was to have hundreds of workmen build a massive wooden barrier to dam the river. In the meantime, hundreds more workmen would dig like fury and create a canal into which the river would flow and be diverted around Pisa.

Outcome: Unfortunately for Leonardo (but fortunately for the Pisans) all sorts of irritating stuff, like lack of manpower and collapsing canal banks, got in the way of the scheme and, after six months of digging, the project was abandoned.

Super-brainwave two: Cutting-edge canal

Leonardo wanted to link Florence to the sea by creating a canal that would either climb hills by a series of giant steps controlled by locks and pumps or that would flow through a tunnel cut through the rocks. Ships would sail along this canal and all the way along it there would be silk mills, saw mills, paper mills, potters' wheels and stacks more water-powered machines.

Outcome: Leonardo's canal was never built but, in the twentieth century, the Italians did make that tunnel through the hills, for the Florence to Pisa motorway.

Super-brainwave three: Lock 'em out

In 1500, the Venetians were threatened by a huge Turkish army which was camped on the banks of the Isonzo river, about 50 miles away from their city. Leonardo had the idea of damming the river further upstream with a portable wooden lock in order to create a huge build-up of water. Then, when the Turks crossed the river to attack Venice, the lock gates would be opened, releasing millions of gallons of water that would go rushing down the valley and drown the whole lot of them in one go.

HEY, MUSTAPHA! DIG THE CRAZY BOOGIE BOARD!

Outcome: The Venetians put the dampers on Leonardo's idea and the Turks stayed high and dry.

Leo's miraculous watery reflections

As well as dreaming up schemes to take advantage of water's phenomenal power, Leonardo also worked out new ideas simply by observing the way it behaved in different circumstances...

Reflection one: Wonder waves

While he was watching the action of waves on water, in his own super-brainy way, he suddenly thought that light and sound might travel through the air in a similar manner! Today the idea of light and sound waves are integral to much of our advanced technology.

124

Reflection two: Steaming ahead

He looked at a pot lid on boiling water and saw that it was bobbing up and down almost as if an invisible hand was pushing it. From this he worked out that boiled

water expands as steam. A fact that Thomas Savery would cotton on to 200 years later when, realizing that expanding steam had real pushing-power, he went on to invent the first steam engine.

Reflection three: Pond pondering

He threw two stones into a pond and noticed that the sets of rings that appeared to spread outwards from the spot where the stone had plopped in didn't actually break up or intersect.

Then he had a little think and worked out that although the water seemed to be moving it wasn't doing much moving at all. What in fact was happening was that a sort of trembling motion was transmitted through the water and this was giving the appearance of movement.

And of course, in addition to his schemes and observations concerning water, Leonardo had a torrent of ideas for inventions linked to H_2O. Like these...

The dynamic diving suit

As well as dreaming up the idea for what some people describe as the world's first submarine, Leo also designed this diving suit made from watertight animal skin.

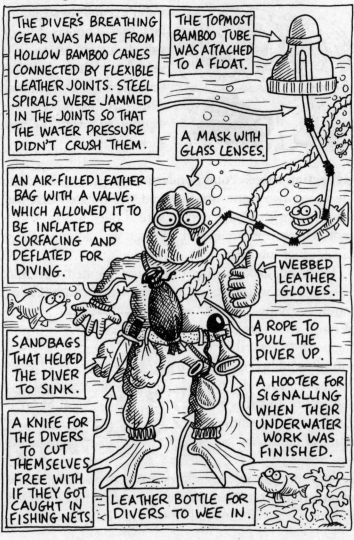

THE DIVER'S BREATHING GEAR WAS MADE FROM HOLLOW BAMBOO CANES CONNECTED BY FLEXIBLE LEATHER JOINTS. STEEL SPIRALS WERE JAMMED IN THE JOINTS SO THAT THE WATER PRESSURE DIDN'T CRUSH THEM.

THE TOPMOST BAMBOO TUBE WAS ATTACHED TO A FLOAT.

A MASK WITH GLASS LENSES.

AN AIR-FILLED LEATHER BAG WITH A VALVE, WHICH ALLOWED IT TO BE INFLATED FOR SURFACING AND DEFLATED FOR DIVING.

WEBBED LEATHER GLOVES.

SANDBAGS THAT HELPED THE DIVER TO SINK.

A ROPE TO PULL THE DIVER UP.

A HOOTER FOR SIGNALLING WHEN THEIR UNDERWATER WORK WAS FINISHED.

A KNIFE FOR THE DIVERS TO CUT THEMSELVES FREE WITH IF THEY GOT CAUGHT IN FISHING NETS.

LEATHER BOTTLE FOR DIVERS TO WEE IN.

One of Leonardo's big ideas was for divers wearing these outfits to plunge into the waters of enemy harbours then sabotage and sink their ships by drilling massive great holes in their hulls (he designed the drills, too).

Water-pipe hollowing gizmo

Nowadays, our water flows through plastic or metal pipes, but in sixteenth-century Italy water mains were made out of massive logs with holes bored through the middle. No matter how thick the log, it was really difficult to keep the hole going straight down the middle of the wood. Leonardo designed an adjustable drill guided by several chucks that made sure the axis of the machine doing the boring stayed in the very centre of the log all the time. The machine looks just like a modern lathe.

Walking-on-water outfit

Leonardo also dreamed up this outfit for walking on water (and saving a fortune in cross-Channel ferry fees). However, as far as we know, he never got round to making it or testing it.

Devising diabolical schemes to drown the Turks and dry out the city of Pisa weren't Leonardo's only involvements in the conflicts of his country. He was soon going to become entangled in the awful affairs of some of the cruellest and most ruthless Italians in history...

DODGY DUDES
AND CRUEL CONTRAPTIONS

Leonardo was soon back on the move again and this time he decided to return to the nearest thing he had to a home city: Florence. While he'd been away, Florence had changed – big time. And one of the people responsible for the changes was this fifteenth-century party-pooper...

Girolamo Savonarola (1452–1498)
Savonarola was a fanatical Florentine friar who wandered around the city preaching to huge crowds of people and yelling...

THE MEDICI ARE A BUNCH OF CORRUPT NO-GOOD WASTERS!

IT'S NOT GOOD TO HAVE FUN. GOD WILL PUNISH YOU!

KNOCK KNOCK JOKES ARE THE WORK OF THE DEVIL!

In addition to being fanatically religious, Girolamo also believed he could see into the future and was forever predicting doom and gloom, saying that one day a great foreign army would come and punish the people of Florence for being such irresponsible Renaissance ravers. Amazingly, in 1494, his prophecy came true and, as you've discovered (see page 99), a stonking great army, led by King Charles VIII of France, did come storming into Italy. As the French marched south, the citizens of Florence drove out the Medici and set up a self-governing republic with Girolamo acting as their adviser on matters relating to all things holy. He promptly informed them that God didn't want them doing things like wearing nice clothes and eating that really sinful stuff known as *food* and, to get back in his good books, they should starve themselves for days on end and dress in bin liners instead of silks and furs (well, almost!). The things that Girolamo is best remembered for are his Bonfires of the Vanities. These involved him getting the Florentines to bung all of their fave goodies such as antiques, jewellery, paintings, musical instruments, soap, books, make-up, mirrors and playing cards on to enormous public bonfires because having possessions of this sort was considered really wicked and evil.

After a while, the Catholic church and various other powerful bods, who had initially put up with Girolamo, decided that he was going a bit far with his clean-up campaign (especially when he criticized the Pope for being a self-indulgent layabout). After being thoroughly tortured he was thoroughly hanged, then given his very own Bonfire of the Vanities when he was thoroughly burned at the stake in Florence in 1498.

DO YOU THINK WE OUGHT TO SHOOT HIM NOW? JUST TO MAKE SURE?

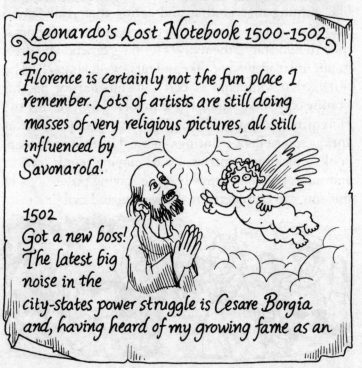

Leonardo's Lost Notebook 1500–1502

1500

Florence is certainly not the fun place I remember. Lots of artists are still doing masses of very religious pictures, all still influenced by Savonarola!

1502

Got a new boss! The latest big noise in the city-states power struggle is Cesare Borgia and, having heard of my growing fame as an inventor of fiendish devices, he's just made me his military engineer. Young Cheesy, as I like to call him (but behind his back, of course!), is the Pope's son and a real go-getter who's currently using his daddy's army to try and take over a huge chunk of Italy. The top dogs in Florence want to stay on the right side of him so they've sort of loaned me to him on account of my general brilliance and usefulness. He's really ruthless and dangerous so I'll certainly try and stay in his good books. At the moment him and me, not to mention several thousand of his terrifying troops, are wandering around central Italy, doing a lot of battling here and a bit of besieging there. I've seen some very violent and bloody stuff taking place. But I don't think I really want to write about it here. Well, I am a pacifist!

Cesare Borgia (1476–1507)

Cesare was good looking, witty and intelligent. However, he was also a murderous, scheming, evil, treacherous and cruel monster ... and that was on his good days. Amongst the many wicked things he is said to have done is having his own brother murdered and dumped in the River Tiber, bumping off the various princes his sister got married to, and murdering anyone else he couldn't trick or bribe into going along with his evil plans for power and wealth. At one point, when some of his soldiers rebelled against him, he said he would agree to all their demands and suggested they should have a chummy pow-wow to discuss them. Then, when they turned up at the meeting, he had the whole lot strangled.

As well as being a thoroughly bad lot, Cesare was also a bit unusual in his habits. He went to bed in the morning, ate his brekky at four in the afternoon and had two pet leopards, which he regularly took hunting with him.

He once also, single-handedly, killed five huge bulls in St Peter's Square in Rome, which is said to have amused the watching crowds no end (but thoroughly upset the bulls). His general ambition was to take over all of central and southern Italy. Fortunately for the people of Italy, when Cesare's father, Pope Alexander VI, died Cesare's own power quickly declined.

He spent his last years in virtual obscurity, suffering from a horrible disease, only moving about at night and always wearing a black mask to cover the huge, dribbly sores that now covered his once handsome face (ha! That'll teach him).

War ... or peace?

A lot of people have since been puzzled by Leo's links to the warlike and bloodthirsty Cesare, especially as he once said: 'Men who go to war are nothing but mad beasts!' He regularly claimed that he detested war and all the painful, nasty stuff that went with it. Despite discussing this puzzling attitude until the cows come home and doing all sorts of investigations, no one's quite managed to come up with an answer to these strange contradictions in Leo's personality. However it could well be that, like so many people (including *you*, reader!), Leo was simply a mixture of good and bad!

Leo's people-pulverizers

Leonardo certainly didn't seem to have any doubts about using his super-brain to devise death-dealing machines. And that, of course, was one of the main reasons that power-hungry politicians like Cesare Borgia and Duke Ludovico were attracted to him.

The amazing tank-u-crank

During the fifteenth century, warfare changed quite dramatically because old weapons, like swords, spears, bows and arrows were being replaced by far more destructive new ones, like dirty great blunderbusses and huge cannons. With cannonballs the size of watermelons, you could bash through castle walls and blow off a man's head quicker than they could say...

In order to give soldiers protection from all these nasty missiles and bombs, Leonardo dreamed up an amazing armoured car, which many people have described as the world's first-ever tank. However, Leonardo didn't call it that, he said it was: 'A covered chariot which is safe and cannot be assaulted.'

Leonardo's tank design looked like an enormous metal meat pie on wheels. It was intended to go charging through the enemy ranks, scattering them, whilst giving cover to the soldiers who charged along behind it. Just to make sure that the enemy knew that these tanks meant terror, gunners in

the upper conical turret would fire through slits as they made their advance.

The tank, which was protected by metal plates, would be powered by eight men who would crouch inside it, rotating a crank that turned the wheels. At one point Leo did actually think of having horses inside the tank

instead of men, to propel it into battle simply by galloping. In the end he decided against this idea because he thought the horses wouldn't be too happy squashed up in such a confined space and the noise of battle would cause them to panic.

It was more than four centuries before someone got round to making the tanks that soldiers know and loathe today. The first tanks went into action in 1916 at the Battle of the Somme in the First World War and, surprise, surprise, they were used just as Leonardo had first suggested, with the tanks advancing across the battlefield, destroying all in their path, while troops trotted behind them, using them as protection from enemy fire. So, as with so many of his inventions, Leo and his super-brain had come up with an idea that was hundreds of years ahead of its time!

The seriously scary scythed chariot

This is the sort of cutting-edge fifteenth-century battle technology that makes thighs cry and kneecaps weep! There were already a few scythed chariots about before the fifteenth century but Leonardo's design was a sort of upgrade and variation on the ones that already existed. The idea was that, as the chariot charged into the opposing masses, the scythes would spin furiously, rapidly transforming the enemy troops into heaps of mini-kebabs. However, there was one big drawback to the scythed chariot. Sharp-witted Leonardo saw it in a flash. Can you? Was it…

a) The enemy soldiers could bung huge, feather-covered rubber bungs on to the blades, thus turning them into giant tickling-sticks.

b) The enemy soldiers could use a really skilful, high-energy skipping routine, and therefore manage to avoid the vicious scythes.

c) The enemy soldiers could force your own soldiers into a painful meeting with the chariot.

Answer: **c)** Leonardo said that enemy generals could turn this weapon to their own advantage by getting their troops to shout and bang drums so that the scythed chariot horses turned round and ran back at their own soldiers, chopping them up in the process.

The really 'arrowing colossal crossbow

Crossbows had been a really big hit during the Middle Ages, but had recently been outclassed by longbows and outpowered by various sorts of guns. Leonardo's idea was that this daddy-of-all-crossbows would fire giant arrows into ranks of enemy soldiers, creating terror and panic.

The multi-barrel machine gun

Leonardo designed this machine gun some time between 1480 and 1482. It was actually 33 small guns lined up in three rows of 11. The guns were fired one at a time. Leonardo described them as barrelled organs because the barrels looked like organ pipes.

Leonardo's Lost Notebook 1502

Still busy being Cesare's military engineer And I've just worked out a way of discovering if someone's trying to tunnel underneath you. Could be useful, as enemy forces frequently try and mine their way under our defences. What you do is put a drum on the ground then put some dice on the drum-skin. If the dice jump about you know that some sort of subterranean activity is taking place because they're responding to the vibrations! Something else I've been thinking about recently, along with sound, is light. I've noticed that you see the smoke from a gun before you hear the explosion and that you see lightning before you hear thunder. Which can only mean one thing. Light travels faster than sound! There's just so much we don't know about the world we live in!

BOINK! BOINK!

FLASH!

BANG!

(a few months later)

I'm busy travelling around checking out the fortifications of Cesare's various strongholds, making maps and dreaming up new ways to defeat his foes. Young Cheesy's given me a special passport that says I can go wherever I please and whoever I meet must help me in my work. I must say I'm rather enjoying the map-making. This is one I drew of Central Italy.

The other day I met this strange little whippet of a bloke. He's called Machiavelli and he's one of the movers and shakers in the new Republic of Florence. He's obviously very impressed by my Borgia boss. And I'm getting on with Machiavelli rather well!

Niccolò Machiavelli (1469–1527)

Leo's new pal, Niccolò Machiavelli, was an official in the new Medici-free Republic of Florence. He looked like a cross between a ferret, a Mekon and a bacon slicer and became known for being so dodgy and crafty that even nowadays his name is used to describe people who are wicked, scheming and untrustworthy.

When he wasn't busy scheming or sucking up to Cesare Borgia and helping him with his wicked plans for pan-Italian domination, Niccolò spent his time working on his book, which he called *The Prince*. Much of it was based on the life of Cesare and in it Niccolò suggested that, rather than wearing open-toed sandals and being kind to lost kittens, it was OK for rulers to keep control by being dishonest, ruthless and cruel, as a firm hand, even with the odd bit of creative torture, led to stable and happy societies.

Ever since *The Prince* was published it's been required reading for thugs and bullies the world over, including Napoleon Bonaparte, who said it was the only book worth reading (apart from *Asterix the Gaul*).

The triple-chance lance

Instead of a horseman simply kebabbing one enemy soldier, Leonardo invented this triple-spear arrangement so that he could skewer a whole barbecue full in one go! The cavalryman held one lance in his hands and the other two were attached to his saddle.

The siege ladder pusher-offer

During medieval and Renaissance times, having your castle besieged by bloodthirsty enemies was a constant problem. To sort out these anti-social climbers, Leo invented this thingy for pushing their ladders away from castle walls. However, to save lots of rushing around, he designed his clever gizmo so that it would push away at least five siege ladders at once!

The rather surprising sword-snatching shield

As your opponent thrust his weapon at you and it made contact with your shield, a door would open in the face of the shield and a sort of trap would jump out and seize the sword from your enemy's hand.

Fortunately for Leonardo, the beastly Borgia was only his boss for a short time. When Cesare's famous dad finally 'Poped' his clogs, Cesare fled to Spain to escape all the people he'd upset during his reign of terror. So Leo stopped working for him and not long after that he returned to Florence. Which was where he was to encounter the young artist who would turn out to be his biggest rival of all time...

THE FRESCO KID

In 1503, Florence was at war with Pisa (yes, again!). Leonardo's hair and beard had turned white and, at the age of 51, he was considered to be a real oldy. While he'd been away doing his thing in Milan and other parts of Italy, many up-and-coming young artists had made their mark in Florence. And, despite the fact that many of these artists had been knee-high to a pencil sharpener when Leo was doing his stuff back in the 1470s, several of them were now so successful that they'd become his professional rivals. His number one thorn-in-the-side amongst all of these whippersnappers was the mega-famous and super-stroppy...

Michelangelo Buonarroti (1475–1564)

Michelangelo was a brilliant sculptor, architect, fresco painter and poet and, just like Leonardo, he'd done his training in a master artist's workshop in Florence. When he was still quite young he was spotted by Lorenzo di Medici, who decided that Michelangelo was so talented that he took him to live and work at his house. Later in his career, Michelangelo went to Rome where Pope Julius II set him to work on prestigious projects such as designing him a snazzy new tomb and carving the *Cross-Legged Captive*, a marble sculpture of a slave.

In contrast to his amazing sculptures of magnificently muscled, tall heroes and beautiful Biblical characters, Michelangelo was short, stocky and scruffy. He had a crooked nose, which he'd broken during a punch-up with another sculptor, and was an argumentative sort who would fight at the drop of a chisel. But he was incredibly industrious and so devoted to his work that he slept in his studio, making do with the occasional crust of bread and jug of wine and never, ever, bothering to wash or even take off his favourite boots, which for some reason known only to him, were made from dog skin.

One of Michelangelo's best-known creations is the huge statue of *David*, the sure-shot shepherd boy, which he sculpted from a block of marble that had been botched by another sculptor and was so massive that no one else had the nerve to do anything with it.

However, Michelangelo's most famous work is the ginormous set of pictures he painted on the ceiling of the Sistine Chapel in Rome, which show stories from the Book of Genesis in the Bible, including the creation of the world. The ceiling is the size of six football pitches and, as moan-a-minute Michelangelo sacked all of his assistants because he thought they weren't up to the job, it took him four years to complete, during which time he stood on scaffolding and painted onto wet plaster in the fresco method.

Man-of-the-moment Michelangelo was often given jobs that Leo fancied for himself and this of course made him jealous to bits of his mega-talented and youthful rival.

Leonardo didn't have a very high opinion of sculptors either and, although he realized the art of sculpting did have some good points, he thought painting was a more appealing sort of activity...

Leo's gems of wisdom: sculpture vs painting

Sculpting: On the plus side, I've got to admit that nothing lasts nearly as well as marble or bronze as far as materials are concerned. But that's about it! Sculpture isn't a patch on painting. I mean it's all...

And there's hardly any thinking to do. It just wears you out and makes you dirty. Sculptors get out of breath, they sweat and then the dust gets stuck all over them and they end up looking like bakers covered in flour, or like they've been out in a blizzard.

And, what's more, their homes are ankle-deep in rubble from all that chipping and hacking.

Painting: Now you're talking! It's a joy. Such a *brainy* sort of activity! And you can do it sitting in a comfy chair and wearing your best clothes. Your paintbrushes aren't a bit heavy and you get to dip them in lovely colours. You live in a clean house and can have music while you work. Or someone reading to you if you feel like it. No contest!

Punch-up in the piazza

One day Leonardo and an artist friend were strolling across a beautiful Florentine piazza when some people who were sitting on a bench, chatting about art and whatnot, stopped the great man and asked him for his opinion about some poetry. Just at that instant, who should come storming across the piazza but moody Michelangelo himself. Instead of answering the question, Leonardo pointed to Michelangelo and said something like:

HERE COMES MICHELANGELO. HE'LL TELL YOU WHAT'S WHAT!

Being in rat-bag mode, as usual, the stroppy sculptor immediately assumed that Leonardo was making fun of him and said something like:

YOU TELL THEM, BIG-BRAINS! YOU'RE THE ONE WHO MADE THE CLAY HORSE MODEL THAT YOU COULDN'T CAST IN BRONZE AND HAD TO BOTTLE OUT OF MAKING, FUNGUS-FACE!

Leonardo was so gobsmacked at this insult that he blushed pinker than his famous pink robe, but before he

147

could think up a suitably witty reply Michelangelo charged off, just pausing long enough to look over his shoulder and add:

AND JUST TO THINK! THOSE POOR SCHMUCKS IN MILAN THOUGHT YOU COULD HACK IT!

Or words to that effect. This naturally upset Leonardo even more.

The big boys 'battle' it out!

Later in 1503, Niccolò Machiavelli and the other big cheeses of Florence decided to get the two top artists of their day to each paint a stonking great battle scene on opposite interior walls of the Grand Council Chamber. Niccolò did his mate a big favour by putting Leonardo's name forward as one of the chosen painters and, of course, the other top-dog artist selected for the job was the moody-man in the pooch-skin footwear.

DRAW!

Leonardo was asked to paint a huge mural to commemorate the Battle of Anghiari, at which the Florentines had knocked the stuffing out of the Milanese. On the other wall Michelangelo was asked to paint the Battle of Cascina, where the Florentines had pulverized some Pisans who'd just whipped their kit off prior to a refreshing frolic in a river.

So that he could get the scene just right, Leonardo got a full description of the battle from a military official. This listed all the gory details, including the numbers of soldiers involved, the huge amounts of casualties, the heroic defence of a crucial bridge and the reported guest appearance of St Peter in the clouds above the punch-up (obviously checking to see how busy his Big Gate was likely to be in the coming days and weeks).

However, another official later reported that the battle had actually involved only one casualty (and that was a really clumsy soldier who'd managed to fall off his horse). As twits falling off horses isn't really the stuff of gigantic, breathtaking battle panoramas, Leonardo decided to go for the big, action-packed picture option with masses of soldiers scrapping and a cavalry battle in the centre.

And the floppy bits, too!

Leonardo took two years preparing his sketches for the Anghiari battle painting and he spent lots of that time at Santa Maria Nuova hospital in Florence. But not because he was ill! As you know, Leonardo was chronically curious. And as a result of his insatiable need to know, he was forever thrusting his nose into places where other folk wouldn't dream of putting theirs ... including the squidgy, floppy, twangy, dribbly bits of other people's bodies, but normally after they'd died!

This was partly because, like many artists including Michelangelo, he believed that you couldn't properly sketch and paint the human figure unless you really understood which bit did what, the shape of the bones and muscles, how they were all joined up, how they moved and what lay beneath the surface.

Leonardo was fascinated with the workings of the incredible soft-machine known as the body and was desperate to discover what made it all tick, throb, squirt, jump and jerk.

Learning with Leo

Anatomy: Now, if you're a painter, you need to know how people are put together. If you don't, your paintings of people's bodies will look all wooden and stiff, and people inspecting your art will think they're looking at a bundle of radishes, rather than the incredible, wondrous work of nature known as the human body.

Altogether, during his lifetime Leonardo is thought to have cut up and thoroughly explored at least 30 human bodies. He dissected masses of organs, including lungs, hearts and brains. He also took bones to pieces to find out which sort are hollow, which sort are full of marrow and which sort are spongy. As a way of trying to understand the mechanics of our bodies, i.e. the way we move, he actually replaced muscles with lengths of string, which he tweaked and tugged in order to imitate the way the tendons pull our bones.

And in order to draw the organs, which tended to flop and droop once they'd been removed, he'd wash them, then inject them with wax so they'd assume their original shape.

As well as studying the bodies of humans, Leo also took a serious in-depth look at the corpses of creatures including bears, cows, frogs, monkeys and birds, so that he could compare them to human bodies and identify their similarities and differences.

Leonardo did at least 200 illustrations of the human body. Most are incredibly accurate, although some are completely inaccurate and simply made up. Leo's anatomical drawings are also incredibly beautiful and many of them take pride of place in art collections around the world.

The imaginative ways he presented the things he found out caught on and were used by later illustrators. In order to display the various layers of our bodies he developed the drawing technique known as the cross section, which medical students still use to this day. He also drew various organs to show every feature from three angles...

Talking about his work on the body, Leonardo once said: 'I want to work miracles.' However, at the end of his anatomical investigations he more or less said that, despite all he'd discovered, he was actually more baffled than ever and that the miracle of human existence was all too mysterious for words. He also said that the thing he'd really been hoping to find was the human soul and that he'd been looking forward to writing down exactly what it was. However, as you'd expect, his quest proved to be entirely fruitless.

When he'd completed the preliminary studies for the battle painting, Leonardo put together a stonking great preparatory cartoon made up of masses of glued-together sheets of paper and, on 6 June 1505, he was finally ready to start the real thing. Then, climbing up his trusty scaffolding, he began to apply paint to the walls that had previously been prepared and smoothed by his little team of helpers. Unfortunately though, just as he slapped on his first brushstroke, the weather decided to have a temper tantrum and in no time at all it was chucking it down. Water went absolutely everywhere, including the spot where Leonardo was painting. As everything got wetter and wetter, all the stuck-together paper bits of the cartoon fell apart.

Nevertheless, a few weeks later Leonardo was ready to have another bash at the picture and began painting again. This time it wasn't the weather that whupped him. It was the wall. After he'd slapped on his first colours, Leonardo decided to light a big coal fire beneath the mural to help his paints dry more quickly. Unfortunately, for technical reasons to do with the oil paints, all the paint in the top part of the picture began to dribble down the wall.

In May 1506, Leo finally realized he was banging his head against a thick wall and stopped battling it out with his big battle picture. In the meantime, Michelangelo had also abandoned his own big punch-up pic. This wasn't because of technical difficulties, though. It was because Pope Julius II was absolutely *dying* for the super-famous sculptor to design him a nice new tomb, not to mention wanting him to do the big makeover job on the ceiling of the Sistine Chapel.

And the winner is…

The big cheeses and top tomatoes of Italy continued to ask Michelangelo to create all the really important works of the day. And as a result, the young whippersnapper remained a pain in the older artist's increasingly wrinkled neck for the rest of his days, eventually causing him to up painting-sticks and flit to France. However, before that happened Leo would create what was to eventually become the most famous painting in the world, thereby enabling him to have the last laugh (or should that be the last *smile*?).

SMILE!

Some time around 1505, Leonardo started work on an oil painting of a smiling woman. The picture, which now measures 77 cm by 53 cm, is known as the *Mona Lisa* and it is the most famous painting on planet Earth. All sorts of reasons are given for the *Mona Lisa* being such a popular and well-known painting. Some people say it's because her eyes follow you around the room no matter where you stand, others say it's because her lips appear to quiver as you stare at them, and some art experts claim it's because Leonardo's smoky sfumato painting style gives her an air of mystery and excitement. It's said that Leonardo loved this painting so much that he took it with him everywhere he went.

WELL, ALMOST...

He eventually sold it to Louis XII, the King of France, after which the *Mona Lisa* spent her time hanging around posh palaces and magnificent mansions until the French Revolution, when the revolting masses transferred her to the Louvre art gallery in Paris. When Napoleon came to power he took her out of the Louvre and hung her in his own bedroom.

Since Leonardo painted her, the *Mona Lisa's* been copied thousands and thousands of times. She's had her mush slapped on tins of Mona Lisa brand tomatoes, appeared on cocktail napkins, jigsaws, holograms and countless other nicknacks and household objects. She's even been featured on those blocks of air freshener that people bung down their toilets.

No one's quite sure who the woman, Mona Lisa, actually was. Many art experts seem to think she was the wife of a rich merchant called Francesco del Giocondo, which is she why she's often referred to as *La Gioconda*. However, other arty know-it-alls have said she may well have been some sort of high-class sixteenth-century lady of the kind that rich Italian men liked to be seen swanning around with. Other people have even said she could have been Leonardo's mum! The thing that really drives people nuts about the *Mona Lisa* is the mysterious smile that plays around the corners of her mouth.

In portraits in those days people were normally pictured with stern, unsmiling faces (usually their own). So why was the Mona Lisa smirking? Some people have suggested it's because Leonardo employed musicians, comedians and storytellers to entertain her while he was painting her. Others have said that the picture is actually a self-portrait painted by Leonardo wearing a wig and grinning at his own joke. Someone else has claimed that Mona Lisa is wearing dentures and that her strange smile is the result of her efforts to stop them falling out.

The low-down on the *Mona Lisa*

• In 1919, a famous French artist called Marcel Duchamp painted a copy of the *Mona Lisa* sporting a cute moustache and a cheeky goatee beard. He called the picture L.H.O.O.Q. Spoken out loud this sounds like, 'Elle a chaud au cul' which means, 'She's got a hot bottom.' (Artists – you can't take them anywhere!)

• In 1983, a Japanese artist called Tadahiko Okawa made his own version of the *Mona Lisa*. But not in oils. He created her out of 1,436 pieces of toast. Yes, really!

159

He sketched her out on aluminium foil, cut out the pieces of foil, then put an appropriately shaped piece of bread on each of them. After carefully toasting each section of the picture until it had achieved just the right degree of browness, he assembled the lot to create his crunchy masterpiece.

- Mona Lisa was originally flanked by two stone pillars, which were part of the window she was sitting at. For some reason, someone sawed about 6 cm from each side of the painting so the pillars disappeared. They've never been seen since. (Wooden you think they could have found something else to light the stove with?)

- Amongst the hundreds of other versions of the *Mona Lisa* that have been painted, she has been featured: a) sitting on a motorbike in her underwear; b) as a gorilla, title: *Mona Gorilla*; c) in her curlers; d) peeping out of a window at film star Clint Eastwood as he stands in the main street of a Wild West town wearing a mean expression … and nothing else.

- In 1911, an Italian working at the Louvre swiftly stuffed the *Mona Lisa* up his smock and ran off with her. The theft shocked people so much that thousands of them rushed to the Louvre to stare at the empty bit of wall where the picture had previously hung. The *Mona Lisa* was eventually recovered two years later but not before con-artists had flogged no less than *six* 'original' *Mona Lisas* to unsuspecting Americans, claiming each one of them to be the stolen masterpiece.

- An attendant in the Louvre became so obsessed with the *Mona Lisa* that he regularly had long chats with her, and got really jealous when the tourists looked at her because he thought she gave them an extra big smile. Not long afterwards, he was 'retired' from his job.

- The *Mona Lisa* still lives at the Louvre, where she's got a gallery all to herself. But she never gets lonely. She gets over 20,000 visitors every day!

Fifteenth-century art-itudes

We may not know where the *Mona Lisa* really got her smirk from but we can be sure about one thing. Like all of Leonardo's pictures, she was certainly a commissioned painting. In other words, someone asked him to paint the picture and promised to pay him for his work.

During the early Renaissance, artists were simply seen as skilled craftspeople, just like plumbers, shoemakers, or carpenters, whose job it was to create beautiful works of art for anyone who was rich enough to commission them.

Quite frequently, pictures and other creations were joint efforts created by two or more artists, and Renaissance artists usually didn't sign their work. Consequently several 'Leonardo's' are actually pictures which were drawn by Leonardo, then painted by him and one or more of his mates.

However, during the Renaissance, artists like Leonardo, Michelangelo, Raphael and Titian achieved such widespread fame as a result of all their great work that they began to be seen as much more than just craftsmen. This was the beginning of a change in attitude towards artists that would eventually lead to the artist-as-sensitive-creative-celebrity-oh-look-at-me-aren't-I-special-flounce-flounce-flounce status that several (thousand) arty types assumed in later centuries.

Have YOU got a Leonardo in your loft?

Despite the fact that Leonardo worked his socks off at his pictures, there are only 27 or so pictures painted by him (or him and a mate) in the whole world. And of these, only 12 were definitely painted solely by Leonardo. Well, they're the ones that people know about! As he never signed or titled his paintings there's no telling how many lost da Vinci masterpieces are out there, covered in dirt, being used as TV dinner trays, draught excluders, or chicken-house roofs. So next time you're ferreting around at the local car boot sale, keep your eyes skinned, you might just strike lucky, like this bloke did...

Around about 1480, Leonardo painted a picture of St Jerome (the fourth-century hermit and Bible translator) sitting at the mouth of a cave, looking extremely cheesed off (which isn't surprising as he's furiously clobbering himself with a large rock). He's also being ogled by a really hungry-looking lion, which obviously isn't the least bit grateful for the fact that St Jerome's just pulled a thorn out of its paw.

No one really knows what happened to the picture after Leonardo stopped working on it, but he definitely didn't finish it off properly. About 350 years later, Napoleon Bonaparte's uncle (yes, really), was wandering down a street in Rome when he happened to glance into a junk shop. Tucked away at the back of the shop was a little cupboard with a rather odd-looking door panel, so Napoleon's uncle decided to check it out.

On closer examination he saw that the door panel was actually a painting of the head of a really miserable-looking bloke who seemed to be rather partial to bashing himself up with big rocks. '*Zut alors!*' he thought, 'I reckon this could be part of a lost Renaissance masterpiece.' It was! At some time in the past, some idiot had actually cut off St Jerome's head to mend their bit of broken furniture. Boney's uncle quickly bought the cupboard, then set about looking for the rest of the picture. After months and months of searching he found it in a cobbler's shop, also in Rome. No, it hadn't been turned into a pair of clogs! The cobbler had actually nailed it to his workbench. So, St Jerome was finally united with his scrawny body and his ungrateful lion.

HIGH AMBITIONS AND LOOPY LARKS

In 1505, around the time he was putting a smile on the face of the *Mona Lisa*, Leonardo wrote a book about the flight of birds. Ever since he'd been a nipper he'd been fascinated by birds and had often watched them, marvelling at the way they managed to stay in the air and zoom around with such apparent ease.

As a result, at several points during his life he became completely bird-brained, and obsessed with the idea of inventing a way for men to defy gravity and swoop and soar across the skies. During the 1490s, after getting into a right old flap about flying and making masses of notes and studying birds' wings and feathers and the actual mechanics of flight, he came to the conclusion that:

A bird is simply an instrument functioning according to the laws of nature. In which case a man can recreate that instrument.

165

He set about trying to do just that. One of his designs was for a four-winged machine that involved the poor pilot furiously turning handles with his hands and feet and pushing a piston up and down with his head.

Had this idea been successful it might have transformed the way we fly today.

Leo's flights of fancy

Leo became so convinced that a man might be able to fly that he eventually began building a model flying machine, but he was so anxious to keep it a secret that he boarded up the windows of his house so no one could pinch his ideas.

At first he thought that attaching a pair of whopping great wings to a man then getting him to flap his arms like mad, would get him off the ground. It's thought that he actually planned to test his machine by jumping off the roof of one of the palaces in Milan, and it's rumoured that one of Leonardo's pupils might have actually taken the plunge for him, but with less successful results than they'd hoped for.

The really screwy flying machine

This is one of Leonardo's most famous futuristic flying inventions, which he designed in the 1480s during his time in Milan. It's often referred to as an early version of the modern helicopter, although he called it an aerial screw device (doesn't sound half as snappy as chopper, does it?). He said:

> *It must be made out of linen cloth, the pores of which have been closed with starch. If the device is promptly reversed, the screw will engage its gear when in the air and it will rise up on high.*

It's thought that his idea was for it to be operated by four men who would stand on the central platform, pushing the bars to make the shaft turn.

The dashed dangerous descent-a-tent

In 1483 Leo drew this picture of a man clinging on to what appears to be a tent. Next to it he scribbled some notes that more or less said that if you give a man 12 metres of cloth and some sticks to hang on to he can jump from any height without hurting himself. This

was Leonardo's design for an early form of parachute, modelled on a tent that Roman soldiers used. As far as is known, no one actually got around to making or testing the parachute, probably because there wasn't a lot of call for that sort of thing in sixteenth-century Italy, what with it being another 400 years before anyone would get round to inventing a working aeroplane to leap out of.

However, in June 2000, a brave British idiot did leap out of the basket of a hot-air balloon wearing an exact copy of Leo's tent parachute. And he survived a 3,000-metre fall, despite having been told by experts that he wouldn't. But he did cheat a bit because if the parachute had been made using authentic sixteenth-century materials it would have been an incredibly heavy 85kg (the weight of a hefty man), and would have squashed him flat when he landed. To avoid this, the plucky plummeter wore a parachute made from modern materials which he opened when he got to 600 metres.

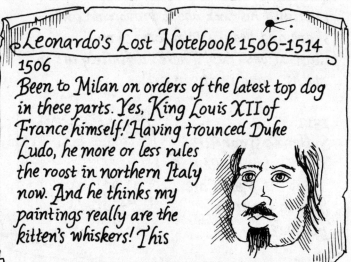

Leonardo's Lost Notebook 1506–1514

1506

Been to Milan on orders of the latest top dog in these parts. Yes, King Louis XII of France himself! Having trounced Duke Ludo, he more or less rules the roost in northern Italy now. And he thinks my paintings really are the kitten's whiskers! This would have cheered me up no end if not for one thing! My poor old Uncle Francesco has just died. As I keep remembering our lovely walks in the hills, my eyes fill with tears.

1508

Been nipping backwards and forwards between Florence and Milan. Designed a room-cooling system for the French governor in Milan. It's run by water which powers a music-making machine at the same time. Hope he goes for it!

1509

Pacioli, my mathematician mate, has just published his book about proportion and shape and beauty with some of my illustrations. Yup! There's definitely art in maths... and maths in art!

1512

Suffering spaghetti! You wouldn't believe it ... but the Medici are back in power in Florence.

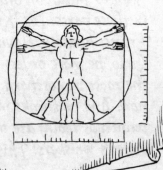

1513

Even more amazing! One of the Medici has just been made Pope! And now he's ordered me to come to Rome.

1514

In Rome. And fed up to my back teeth! Supposed to be working on solar-power mirror and lens designs with two German lads. But they're useless, lazy and bad-tempered. And one of them just loves shooting birds. What a monster! Ah well. At least I can keep myself amused with a few practical jokes.

Leo's potty pranks

As well as being arty and scientific, Leonardo was also fiendishly frolicsome. And, having such a hyperactive imagination, he had no problem dreaming up suitable tricks! Here are a few of the pranks he got up to.

The incredible inflatable intestines

Leonardo got a bull's guts (tum, intestines and suchlike), then cleaned them so that they would fit into the palm of his hand. After sneaking them into a room where a posh get-together was about to take place, he attached their open end to some bellows, which he hid in the next room. When people started to arrive at the do he

171

began pumping the bellows and, as he did, the bull's internal bits began to expand...

NB: Don't try this at home.

The dynamic dragon makeover

Fancying a pet with a difference, Leonardo made some little wings out of scaly skin from dead lizards and snakes, which he then painted with mercury (liquid metal used in thermometers). Next he caught a really big, living lizard and attached the wings to it. Just to make sure the lizard was really loathsome he also gave it some extra-big false eyes, a pair of awesome horns and a snazzy little beard. He then tamed his super shiny dragon and began carrying it about in a big box. Whenever he was in the company of particularly nervous (or stupid) people he would release his astonishing pet and let it run around a bit, causing them all to run off screaming (and you thought Godzilla was a *modern* invention!).

Some fantastic flatulent animals

Using a really thin paste partly made from wax, Leonardo made lightweight, hollow models of various creatures, which he then blew into, inflating them like balloons. After he'd got them good and swollen, he let them go, causing them to fly off in all directions, making rude noises as they went.

And finally, here are three party pieces he is said to have performed:

Leonardo's Last Lost Notebook 1517–1519

Spring 1517

I'm in France! I've been appointed Premier Painter and Architect and Engineer to King Francis himself! It took us three months to get here from Italy. Absolutely exhausting for an old chap like me! We crossed the Alps on the way and what stunning sights we've seen. Eagles soaring above the peaks, huge snakes slithering across the tracks and packs of wolves slinking through the forests! A string of mules carried our chests and trunks full of clothes and stuff along with my drawings, notebooks and three paintings, including old 'laughing girl' herself!

Yes, I've brought the lot! Bye bye, Italy. I'm leaving you for ever!

Summer 1517

King Francis of France has given me a lovely manor house to live in. It's at a place

called Cloux and myself, Salai and Melzi (a
young artist friend of mine) have now moved
in. It's got more than two acres of beautiful
gardens and is connected to the Royal
Chateau by an underground tunnel. The
King pops over for a chat almost every day!
Which is nice. He says I'm his favourite
painter, engineer and architect. Pity I can't
paint any more. Recently my arm's become
paralysed by some sort of illness. Ah well,
that's the price of getting old. But at least I
can still draw a bit! The King says I am the
most cultivated man alive and we regularly
enjoy a good old chinwag by the fire. Today
we were nattering about the soul and exactly
what it is. Pity I couldn't tell him! And more
to the point... he's paying me a whopping
great salary for all this! Can't be bad!

1518
Did the old robotic lion routine for the King
and his chums. I've done it before but these
French aristos love it!
It's this huge
mechanical lion I've
knocked up. It walks a
few paces towards the
guests of honour, stops,

ROAR

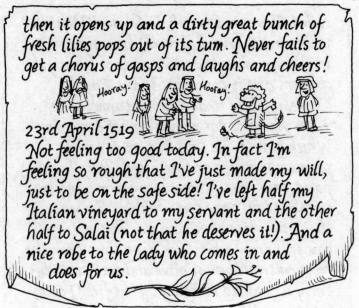

then it opens up and a dirty great bunch of fresh lilies pops out of its tum. Never fails to get a chorus of gasps and laughs and cheers!

23rd April 1519

Not feeling too good today. In fact I'm feeling so rough that I've just made my will, just to be on the safe side! I've left half my Italian vineyard to my servant and the other half to Salai (not that he deserves it!). And a nice robe to the lady who comes in and does for us.

Leonardo died on 2 May 1519, aged 67. He's said to have died in the King's arms (that's the King of France's arms, not the well-known pub). However, as the King is reported to have been many miles away at the time, some people have said that this story may just be a bit of wishful thinking.

EPILOGUE

Leonardo's body was buried in a French chapel which eventually fell into ruin. In 1802, Napoleon ordered that the place should be tidied up. However, the man doing the job emptied the skellies out of their lead-lined coffins, then melted them down to sell (the coffins, not the skellies). The bones were left scattered in the rubble.

Being unfeeling, little ghouls (like all children) the local kids used the bones to play skittles. Later, a gardener slung the remains into a mass grave, but someone decided to sort through them. Selecting a skull that was much bigger than the others, he decided that this

DON'T YOU KNOW WHO I AM?

must have been Leo's, as his huge super-brain wouldn't have fitted the smaller ones. He then put the skull and some bones in a grave with a monument marked with the inscription: HERE LIES WHAT ARE THOUGHT TO BE THE REMAINS OF LEONARDO DA VINCI.

After Leonardo's death, Francesco Melzi returned to Italy, taking the great man's notebooks with him. Salai had already gone back to Milan and is said to have been killed by a crossbow bolt not long afterwards (probably deserved it anyway). After Melzi died, his son began flogging Leonardo's notebooks to anyone who would hand over the dosh and quite soon they were scattered all over the place, often getting lost, nicked or burned.

As a result, for many years, most people knew nothing at all about Leonardo's engineering and scientific work and remembered him only for his painting. It wasn't until the 1800s, when various toffs began seriously searching out the notebooks and putting them in protected collections, that the world began to see Leo in a new light and realize that as well as being a great artist he'd been a great engineer, anatomist, inventor and architect. Suddenly, everyone was waking up to the fact that a sort of super-human had popped into the world back in fifteenth-century Italy. Quite soon, all sorts of highly educated inquisitive types began poking their noses in Leonardo's notes and drawings and being generally gobsmacked by what a phenomenally busy bee he'd been throughout his life!

However, Leo thought differently. In one of the last entries in his notebooks, made just a few days before he died, he says that he's been thinking back on his life and has generally come to the conclusion that God's probably not too pleased with him ... because he hasn't worked on his art nearly as hard as he ought to have done!

Some slacker, that Leonardo!

Index

181

LOOK OUT FOR

⟶

CHURCHILL

HIS FINEST HOURS

Alan MacDonald

CREATE YOUR OWN INVENTIONS

→